How to

Make

Men's Clothes

HOW TO
MAKE
MEN'S CLOTHES

by Jane Rhinehart

Illustrations by B. J. Shewbart

Doubleday & Company, Inc., Garden City, New York
1975

Library of Congress Cataloging in Publication Data

Rhinehart, Jane.
 How to make men's clothes.

 Includes index.
 1. Men's clothing. 2. Tailoring. I. Title
TT575.R45 646.4'3'02
ISBN 0-385-01850-9
Library of Congress Catalog Card Number 74–12706

Contents

How to
Make
Men's Clothes

CHAPTER 1

The "Mystery" of Men's Tailoring

It seems to me the tailors have been shortsighted in keeping their knowledge to themselves. Certainly their attitude is understandable: Nobody handed them their know-how in a nice, concise package. Most of them worked for years as drudge to an established tailor. (Did you ever hear of a young tailor?) But their secrecy has resulted in fewer people being able to make fine clothes —therefore fewer fine clothes to be seen—and ultimately less demand for them. People must be acquainted with quality tailoring before they will pay for it. If you have never seen a beautifully custom-tailored coat, how can you desire one?

The tailor's suppression of his methods has been so successful that most people don't even know there is another world of sewing besides the dressmaking and "tailoring" taught in schools. Over the years the tailor and the dressmaker have gone separate ways, and each has evolved his own distinct approach to sewing. While the dressmaker has been busy *creating* ever newer styles from ever different fabrics, the tailor has been *producing* basically the same style from a narrow range of suitings using ever more efficient techniques. Because the emphasis in tailoring is on production rather than innovation, it is not surprising that the tailor accomplishes his work in a more direct, businesslike manner. He proceeds in thoroughly refined steps that avoid wasted motion.

Applying the dressmaker's way to sewing for a man inevitably results in a disappointing homemade look. If you want to make good-looking clothes for a man—suits, shirts, or what have you—

take a look at traditional men's tailoring techniques. One fully tailored coat and pants will give you an incomparable education in sewing. There is no better way to gain a firm basis for cutting corners in your sewing and for imposing professional touches where they count.

A master tailor today is hard to find, just how hard being obscured by misleading advertising. I recently checked out the thirteen "tailors" in a city of five hundred thousand. Not a single one of them knows how to make a suit! They all have signs that proclaim "fine custom tailoring" or the like, but these men are *salesmen,* not tailors. They take measurements and send them to a factory, where their suit is made in the same assembly line procedure that supplies the ready-to-wear retailer. The suit is mailed to the salesman, who fits it to the customer and marks any adjustments he thinks will improve the fit; then it is returned to the factory for completion. This "made-to-measure" suit is no more personalized than one from a ready-to-wear rack after store alterations. The customer has had the opportunity of choosing the cloth, but any "custom" tailoring is a myth.

A truly custom-tailored suit is superior in materials, workmanship, and fit. It is made of the best-quality suiting—a real tailor won't handicap himself with anything less workable—and of many different kinds of thread and interfacing, each exactly the right strength or weight or crispness for its purpose. A superior suit can't be made from mediocre cloth, mercerized thread, and only one or two interfacings.

While the total effect of quality is unmistakable, there are several marks of good workmanship that are apparent only to an educated eye. The edges are thin and flat, even where several layers of material are enclosed; and the seams are slightly to the underside. The coat is shaped to conform to the wearer. The collar is nowhere flat but slightly convex, and it hugs the wearer's neck in the back. The revers (pronounced "revere," the part of the coat front that is turned over to the outside) echoes the gentle outward curve of the collar; when turned up, it springs back into place. Underneath it the front of the coat can be seen to curve into the fold (the bridle line) so the fold lies close to the chest. All this shaping depends on hand sewing the foundation of the coat. It enables a well-made coat to hold a press while a poorly made one goes slack between pressings.

A good place to observe the quality of the hand sewing on a coat is under the collar. There the stitches are plainly visible because they overcast the edge of the undercollar at the same time they attach it. Another good spot to check is the inside of the armhole where the lining is sewn into place. Those stitches have to be very close together to take the strain they get. A nice custom touch in the same area is perspiration shields that match the lining.

At one time beautifully handmade buttonholes were an indication of overall high quality, but they are now often put into cheaper suits as an easy means of making a suit seem to be better than it is. So don't be led by handmade buttonholes to overrate a suit, especially if a label calls attention to them.

Neither is a "hand-tailored" suit necessarily well made. Such a label means only that at least twenty-one steps in the coat making were done by hand; it says nothing about the level of workmanship.

An almost infallible indication of quality in a man's suit is the manner in which the edge of the coat is stabilized. The best coats are hand sewn about ¼ inch from the edge (around the collar, down the fronts, and at least part way around the bottom) using two strands of fine silk thread in a practically invisible backstitch. When it is well done, this stitching is so hard to see that sometimes the only way you can find it is to squeeze the edge, pushing in opposite directions with your thumb and finger. If the layers won't separate and you can't see any stitches to account for their stubbornness, you can assume they were sewn by an expert.

With all its superiority of materials and workmanship, a custom-tailored suit mainly is set apart by its better fit. It is cut by a pattern based on a dozen or more measurements of the man who is to wear it, and it is fitted personally by the tailor so he can observe and make adjustments for any little quirks of stance or asymmetries (such as one shoulder higher than the other). No "made-to-measure" suit cut in another city from a slightly altered stock pattern, and no altered ready-made suit can be so personalized. The person who sews well is therefore able to offer a level of craftsmanship not readily available, even at high prices.

To sew successfully for a man, you need to know:

What are the best materials for men's clothes?
Where can I get them?
How do I come up with a pattern that fits?
What are men's tailoring techniques?

Don't be too much awed by experience, or rather by your lack of it. Misguided experience can be nothing but the making of bad habits, while a lack of experience can be overcome by knowledge and determination. Given answers to the above questions, anybody who wants to can achieve professional results. Which, of course, is why the tailors are so secretive.

CHAPTER 2

Tools and Stuff

Unless you have been inside a tailor's supply house, you probably have never seen professional sewing tools. There, instead of a dizzying array of new gadgets, you find comparatively few, highly functional but unornamented tools, some suitings, and a large selection of trimmings (tailor's terminology for everything that goes into a garment other than the "outer cloth").

You notice I say "outer *cloth*" and not "fabric." To a tailor the two are not synonymous, and "cloth" is the more general and the more respected. A tailor would never downgrade good wool suiting, or "stuff," which is another proper term for it, by calling it "fabric."

The variety of a tailor's interfacings is especially impressive. There are canvases of cotton, wool, linen, and various combinations of fibers, each woven to the most economical width for its purpose and available in several weights. So, if you order trimmings for an outer cloth you have bought somewhere else, it is a good idea to send along a sample and request interfacings of a compatible weight.

Trimmings in a supply house are consistently better and cheaper than those in the stores. The best outer cloth, on the other hand, costs more no matter where you buy it. Good men's suitings are priced at $15 to $20 a yard and up. I'm talking now about the quality cloth that goes into a $300 to $400 suit, making your cost for such a suit somewhere around $55 to $75. Less fancy suitings for men (in quality and price) can be found in ordinary cloth stores, where they often go through several price reductions because they don't move as fast as women's suitings. By shopping judiciously it is possible to make slacks for less than $5.00 and sportcoats for $15 to $20.

It is definitely in making the more expensive clothes that you realize the greater saving in sewing. Making cheaper dresses and blouses yields negligible savings, according to a Department of Agriculture study, while tailoring women's suits and coats can mean savings of up to 75 percent. Sewing for a man is even more worthwhile: My own observation is that my efforts are worth about four times as much *per hour* when I am tailoring for a man than when sewing simple garments for myself.

Men's suitings are really very special. They have two contradictory qualities, being eminently shapable and at the same time resistant to unintentional shaping, such as bagging of the pants knees. Women's suiting lacks sufficient stability for tailored pants, though it does make up well in a sportcoat. Men's suiting is likewise a poor choice for a fitted skirt; it assumes angles instead of curves and refuses to drape smoothly over the hips. So be sure you know what you are buying. In the absence of identification your best clue is the width to which each is woven. Women's woven suitings are customarily 45 to 54 inches wide, and men's are 58 to 60 inches (30 if handwoven). Both men's and women's doubleknits are 60 inches, but the menswear knit has a harder finish and a lighter weight, without the spongy feel often found in knits designed for women.

Your choice of a supply house is crucial, and an appropriate one is hard to find. There are only a few scattered over the country, and most of them refuse to sell to the public. A further complication is that in the large cities that are cloth centers the supply houses may handle only trimmings and equipment, while the cloth is marketed separately. What you need is one comprehensive, friendly link with the trade, a source of advice as well as supplies. In case there is no such place in your vicinity, here is one I can recommend unconditionally:

Arthur W. Donnerstag
317 South Robertson Boulevard
Beverly Hills, California 90211

Few supply houses have price lists or sample books as such. In your communications it isn't necessary to be formal, but you should make your inquiries as specific as possible. For example:

> We are interested in a winter-weight, high-grade worsted, brown or tan. What do you have?
>
> What outer cloth do you suggest for slacks to go with a coat of this cloth? (sample enclosed)

After the paraphernalia of the dressmaker, the few tools of the tailor appear almost spartan. You will need to add very little to your present sewing equipment to make it adequate for men's tailoring.

When I tailored the first suit for my husband, we lived in a one-room apartment. I did my sewing perched on a kitchen stool with my $25 portable sewing machine on the counter where we also ate. The pedal had to be balanced on the machine's cover on the floor so my foot could reach it. So don't get the idea you need to rent a gymnasium or buy a lot of things before you can tailor.

A SEWING MACHINE is essential, but even an ancient one will suffice. Many of the power machines used by tailors won't sew backwards, let alone zigzag. It is a huge advantage to be able to overcast seam edges by machine, but straight seaming is all you really have to have.

Measuring tools can be no more than a YARDSTICK and a good TAPE MEASURE. If you are more at home with the metric system than with inches, you will want these tools to be printed both ways for easy conversion. A 6-inch metal guage with slide indicator (the kind sold as a SEAM GAUGE or "sewing gauge" at notions counters) makes it easy to get accustomed to the different seam widths of men's tailoring. I also keep an 18-INCH RULER at hand.

If you plan to draft a lot of patterns, you have an excuse to buy a tailor's DRAFTING SQUARE, though for the one pants pattern I recommend in this book it is an unnecessary expense. Similar to an architect's square, it reads in thirds, sixths, halves, fourths, etc., eliminating the arithmetic otherwise involved in pattern making.

A large, flat CUTTING SURFACE of some sort is in order, but unless you have a very large room just for sewing try not to get carried away over the idea of a sewing table. In a small room a sew-

ing table usually has to be placed against a wall, where it promptly
becomes a catchall for things more efficiently stored in a chest of
drawers. To be of value for cutting out, a table should be clear
when you need it and away from walls so you can walk all the way
around it. If your dining table is not large enough as is, you can
lay on it a 4- by 8-foot sheet of plywood or Masonite, which can be
stored upright when not in use. If you can afford to spread out, you
can permanently support your cutting board on saw horses. A
tailor's workroom often has two such "tables" end-to-end, making
enough room to lay out a full 5 yards of cloth—enough for a two-
pants suit.

Eight-inch bent-handle dressmaker SHEARS are the minimal
cutting tool for tailoring. As you acquire skill in handling them,
you will find yourself increasingly held back by the shortness of the
blades. The tailors favor at least 12-inch shears, but that size is too
heavy for most women. The 10-inch shears are just right for me,
and, unless your hands are a lot smaller than average, you too
should be comfortable with them as soon as you adopt a professional style of cutting.

You also need a second pair of SCISSORS, for cutting thread
ends and doing rough trimming and generally for taking the load off
your good shears, which should be reserved for cutting out and for
fine trimming. A good overall length for this second pair is 5 to
6 inches.

PINKING SHEARS properly have a limited usefulness. They
are too fragile for cutting most cloth in double thickness. Their
many-angled blades are easily thrown out of line, causing the
shears to behave as if they were dull. Besides, enclosed seams are
flatter if their edges are straight cut. Pinking shears are useful,
however, for cutting out silk and silk-like linings, which ravel badly
if straight cut.

A RIPPER is a necessity—the kind that has a blunt point for
picking and a cutting edge that is reached by jabbing through a
stitch. Don't take chances with razor blades or pocketknives!

A tailor's IRON—even a new one—looks like an antique. It is
huge, with a control unit awkwardly designed onto it—totally without streamlining and without any steaming feature. It weighs a ton.

Or rather 20 pounds (12 to 16 in the woman's weight), which compared to my 3-pound household iron is a ton. It is not to be managed in the same manner as a household iron, and yet a 100-pound woman who knows how can sling one of these monstrosities around without difficulty. A tailor's iron is absolutely the only effectual pressing agent for men's suitings, and it is the first "big" item you will want to invest in. Start looking for a used one.

These few pressing forms will serve for all your sewing: a pants board, a coat board, and a sleeve board. Their versatility is such that you have no need for a "tailor's" ham, sleeve roll, or press mitt.

The PANTS BOARD is really a general purpose pressing board, flat and rectangular, that rests on a sturdy table (ideally) or on an ironing board. It can be a piece of ¼-inch plywood or Masonite, 4 feet long and 20 inches wide, padded and covered tightly with drill (a cotton cloth such as heavy jeans are made of—order it from a tailor's supply house). The padding can be old blankets or quilts or cotton batting. This simple pressing form is worth whatever trouble you have to go to get it.

You can buy separate COAT and SLEEVE BOARDS, or you can make a very serviceable combination of the two: From ¾-inch lumber or plywood, cut out the two solid-line shapes:

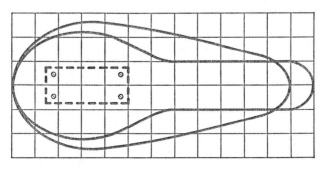

each square = 2 inches

Pattern for coat/sleeve board

The coat board is 24 inches long and the sleeve board is 2 inches longer. Countersink screws to attach the two pieces to opposite sides of a 7-inch length of 4-by-4.

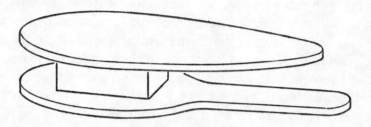

The board assembled

If your inclinations don't run to carpentry, take these instructions to any cabinet shop or lumberyard advertising millwork.

Pad both sides of the board to a well-rounded shape: From the padding cut out a miniature version of the outline of the board, no more than 6 to 8 inches long, and place it on the board. Keep adding layers of padding, each a little larger than the one beneath it (use each preceding piece as a pattern) until you reach a size that extends over the edges of the board. Cut the next larger size from drill, and bind its edge with double-fold bias tape in which you have enclosed a string.

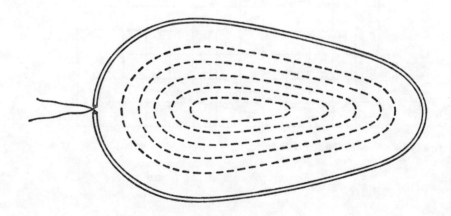

Padding and cover

Draw up the string to make a snug cover for the board. The number of layers depends on the thickness of your padding. Aim for the shape in the illustration, remembering that the pressure of use will flatten it a bit.

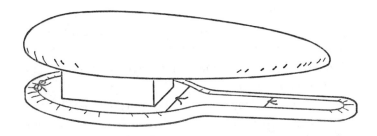

Coat/sleeve board ready for use

When you order the drill (30 inches wide) to cover the pressing forms, buy an extra ¾ yard for a PRESS CLOTH. Wash it thoroughly, and either pink or overcast the edge. Identify the smooth side as "top" or "outside" so you won't have to re-examine it to know which is the rough side, to be placed against what you are pressing.

If you removed all the WAX CHALK from a tailor's shop, you would just about bring everything to a standstill. On a 100 percent wool cloth, wax chalk lines can be completely erased by touching them with a warm iron. So markings can be made safely even on the right side of the work. But this is true only of 100 percent wool. On cloth of any other fiber, wax chalk leaves a grease mark. The CLAY CHALK of the dressmaker is then the choice. These two, wax and clay, are also sometimes called "soft" and "hard" chalk.

Always select SILK PINS. They are better quality and keep their polish longer. It is a good idea to have two boxes of them, one beside the sewing machine and one where you press. Whenever pins no longer penetrate the cloth easily, buy new ones; they are no place to economize. In fact, a tailor who is an astute businessman has computed the time required to pick up a pin from the floor and concluded that his time is worth more if spent in sewing. So any pins that fall to his workroom floor are left lying about, though he will retrieve a needle.

Passing thread across BEESWAX helps to prevent snarls in hand sewing.

Common hand sewing NEEDLES are of three kinds:

> "Sharps" are long and thin and have short eyes. They are a poor design for most sewing, breaking easily and requiring an awkward hand position.
>
> "Crewel" needles are long and have long eyes. They are intended for embroidery, a task for which they are perfectly suited. They are not an all-purpose needle.
>
> "Betweens" are short and stubby with rather fat but short eyes. Unusually strong and well adapted to an easy hand position, they are the hand sewing needles of the tailor.

Sizes of needles range from 1 to 10, the smallest being a 10. About a 3 or 4 is good for basting, and 5 and 6 are right for most permanent sewing on suitings. For linings use the small ones, 9 or 10. I suggest you buy one package in assorted sizes.

The tailor's THIMBLE is open at the end. It is a slightly tapered band of deep grooves that catch the needle firmly. The position of the hand is natural and relaxed—a far cry from the cramped way my mother taught me to hold a needle.

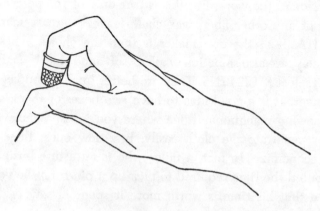

The dressmaker's way

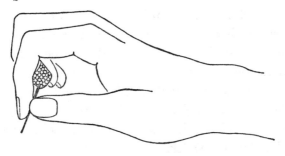

The tailor's way

There is something personal about a thimble. The cheap metal ones do the job all right, but I can't resist suggesting you price the sterling silver ones, which are smoother and such a joy to use. The people I have given silver thimbles are almost as sentimental about theirs as I am about mine, which my husband bought me years ago on our first visit to a tailor's supply house. As for size, the thimble should be even with the end of the finger. Sizing of the tailor's thimbles is the same as for the closed-end dressmaker's thimbles, so you can try on several in a store and come close to the size you should order from a supply house, assuming you can't get what you want locally.

There is one other tool that has become almost indispensable for me. It is a stick of ½-inch-thick solid wood (not plywood) about 6 inches long and 1¼ inches wide with one end squared off and the other pointed. The entire outline is beveled to a single edge.

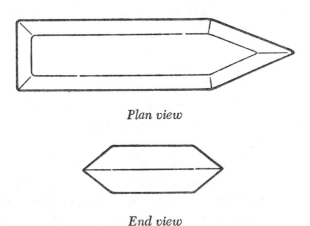

Plan view

End view

This little stick has all the usefulness of an edge board without taking up so much room. You slip it inside a cuff, pocket flap, or other detail that has been sewn up and is to be turned right side out, and press open the seam over the edge of the stick. A seam that has been so pressed will work itself out fully when it is turned, without the irregular tucks that otherwise mar the outline. And any corners can be safely and completely poked out with the slightly dull point of the stick.

Give plenty of deliberation to selection of the OUTER CLOTH for your first pants and coat. The most important consideration is that it be good stuff. Later you will have the ability to get the most from cheaper goods, but your first efforts should not be hampered by an outer cloth that is anything less than the best. There is every reason to expect your first garments to be a success; but, even if you goof, the education fully justifies the cost of good materials.

The best guarantee of a minimum of handling problems is a 100 percent wool—preferably worsted—high-grade *men's* suiting. Anyone who automatically objects at the mention of wool has never come into contact with the best wool suiting, which isn't surprising since the best is reserved for custom tailors. I had to go through an amazing rigamarole before I was allowed to buy from one of the top manufacturers. A supply house will act as go-between for you.

The decline of wool is due primarily to a failure to educate the consumer. None of the man-made textile fibers can measure up to the merits of wool. Cloth from synthetic fibers is not as comfortable to wear because it doesn't "breathe" the way cloth of a natural fiber does. Worse still, synthetic cloth lacks the shaping capability of wool. And perforations and creases are inclined to be permanent in synthetics. So the best suitings are still wool. If you anticipate an objection, get samples first. I have come to expect the "You mean *that* is *wool?*" reaction on first exposure to really good wool suitings.

Wool cloth can be either "woolen" or "worsted," the distinction having to do with the condition of the fibers that make up the yarn. Woolen yarns have been carded but not combed. They are a combination of short and long fibers that lie every which way. Cloths woven from these yarns are relatively soft and have a somewhat fuzzy surface. An example is tweed.

Worsted yarns have been combed to remove the shorter fibers and to cause the remaining long ones to lie parallel. They are comparatively smooth and tightly twisted. Worsted cloths are more firmly woven and have a resilience you can observe by crushing a sample in your hand and watching it spring back wrinkle free. Examples are cheviot, serge, and gabardine. (Sharkskins and flannels may be either woolen or worsted.) Worsteds have excellent shaping capability. Those with a lightly napped surface are easy to press, though perfectly hard finishes, such as gabardine, tend to shine with pressing and wear. The smooother finish of worsted makes it easier to see the stitching, which is an aid to both sewing and ripping. Worsteds are less forgiving of poor workmanship than are woolens, but no other cloth gives so much credit for a job well done.

While you should never compromise on cloth quality in a suit, because only the best suitings have both "shapability" and resistance to stretching, casual pants and sportcoats invite a wider choice of cloth. The reason is that pants and coats each require only one of the contradictory qualities: Nowhere in the making of pants is any shaping required—the construction is all flat. And in a coat you don't have to worry about baggy knees. So for slacks choose almost any firm cloth, and for a sportcoat consider the softer weaves.

Actually, for a coat, I would rather work on tweed than on any other fabric. For easy handling and beautiful pressing it is not to be outdone. It is the most forgiving of fabrics, kindly obscuring slight defects in workmanship. Its economy is noteworthy: The initial price is low, upkeep is minimal, and tweed wears forever. Twelve years ago I made my husband three tweed sportcoats at a cost of about $15 each. For ten years they were the mainstay of his casual wardrobe. These coats just wouldn't give up. In all that time, the only attention I had to give them was to shorten the sleeves when the style changed. Finally the style changed enough that he stopped wearing them, but they still look exactly as they did when they were new. My hesitation to recommend tweed for a first coat therefore calls for an explanation.

The one drawback of tweed is its tendency to ravel. In most sewing this disadvantage is easily got around by overcasting the edges as soon as they are cut. But in tailoring it is often necessary to cut right up to a stitch, and some of the pocket seams are only ⅛ inch wide. Along these seams the loss of just two threads from a loosely woven cloth can destroy your work. One of the advantages of tweed also can work adversely in the hands of a beginner. This is its ability to obscure the stitching, making it hard to see whether you are stitching straight and within the desired limits. If you have had quite a bit of sewing experience and if, being forewarned, you are prepared to preserve every thread intact, then tweed is excellent for a coat. Otherwise, a firmer suiting is a better choice.

Cloth weights are designated in ounces per linear yard. Eight to 10 ounces is summer weight; 11 to 14 is a more or less year-round weight; and anything heavier is winter weight. Overcoats are made of 17-ounce cloth or heavier; a lighter coat is by definition a topcoat rather than an overcoat. The heavier cloths are easier to work with. You should choose at least a 14-ounce cloth at first. Remember that these figures refer to men's suiting. Since the standard is a linear yard, there is a whole different set of figures for the narrower women's suiting. Probably the safest thing is to speak in terms of light, medium, or heavy! In gauging weight, bear in mind that the cloth will seem heavier made up than it does on the bolt or in sample.

The color too should be considered, especially if you do any sewing at night. The lighter shades are easier on your eyes. Avoid black: There is a world of difference between black and even dark gray or navy. Yet it is a help to have a shade dark enough to contrast well with white chalk lines. A solid color or a very small, all-over pattern—one that doesn't require matching—is preferable. And for heaven's sake pick a cloth you *like* so working on it will be a pleasure.

As for yardage, the average amount is 1½ yards for pants and 2 yards for a coat, based on the standard 58- to 60-inch width. Pants in anything narrower than 58 inches call for two full lengths. A coat in 54-inch cloth requires 2 yards plus a sleeve length. Anything in hand-woven cloth, which is half the standard width or 30 inches, naturally takes twice the standard length. (You may want to look into the fabulous hand woven Scottish tweeds for sportcoats.)

Consider these amounts to be an estimate only. As soon as you have your pattern, lay out the pieces and measure exactly how much cloth you require in each of the most common widths—60, 54, 45, and 36 inches. (A rug makes a good surface because the pattern pieces tend to stay put, as does a string to mark the width.)

If you want to begin with a suit, there is no reason you shouldn't; or, if you want to make nonmatching pants and coat, that is an equally good beginning. But whichever combination you choose, the place to begin is with the pants. No matter how much sewing you have done and no matter how eager you may be to make a coat, start with pants. You will see progress faster, and what you learn in making pants will shorten the time it takes to make a first coat. Pants tailoring is elementary—you can get superlative results with the first pair. In fact, it is so easy in comparison with coat making that tailors often hire out their pants making to "pants men" and devote their own expertise exclusively to coats.

One suggestion for when you do make a suit: The life expectancy for pants is much shorter than for coats. With normal wear pants look good for one or two seasons at most, while a well-made coat lasts much longer. This is why many suits come with two pairs of pants. But the style in pants changes more rapidly than in coats. So, when you make a suit, it is wise to buy enough material for two pairs of pants but make only one of them initially. Whenever the suit goes to the dry cleaners, send along the extra pants length of cloth so it will continue to look like the coat. Then, when the first pair of pants wears out, make up the second pair in whatever is the current style.

These are the TRIMMINGS:

For one pair of PANTS:

1½ yards	waistband canvas (strip)
⅝ yard	pants pocketing
½ yard	sateen
⅜ yard	silesia
1	zipper

1	hook and eye
2	buttons
1 yard	linen tape

For a COAT:

2½ yards	lining (39 to 40-inch)
1 yard	hymo (half width)
⅓ yard	haircloth
⅓ yard	white felt
¼ yard	linen canvas
½ yard	wigan
¾ yard	silesia
1	undercollar cloth
1 sheet	wadding
1 set	buttons
4 yards	linen tape

Probably many of these trimmings are unfamiliar to you, and some of them need comment:

WAISTBAND CANVAS is a heavy cotton canvas strip 2¼ inches wide. It can be bought by the yard or by the roll and is good for interfacing all waistbands, skirts as well as pants.

PANTS POCKETING is similar to silesia, described below, but tougher and more leathery to the touch. (In tailor's parlance, it has a leather hand.) It is woven 36 inches wide and comes usually in just two shades, light tan and pearl gray (sometimes also brown and black).

Cotton SATEEN lines the waistband and fly. It comes 40½ inches wide and in the same tan or gray as the pants pocketing. Don't make the mistake I did with my first pants in thinking the beautiful silken coat lining would be elegant as a waistband lining—shirts wouldn't stay tucked in.

Some supply houses now offer a heavier sateen, or lighter pocketing (whichever way you want to look at it), intended for both pockets and waistband lining. I prefer the separate stronger pocketing and thinner sateen for lining when I can find them.

SILESIA is a tough cotton twill (that is, the weave has a diagonal pattern) that comes 36 inches wide and in many colors.

It is used mainly for coat pockets. For pants ⅜ yard is a lot to buy when you need only a few narrow pieces to reinforce the hip pockets, fly, and crotch. But these pieces must be cut lengthwise to take advantage of the warp (lengthwise) strength of the cloth. In the weaving of cloth, the warp threads remain taut while the woof, or filler, goes in and out with a slight amount of slack; therefore, cloth "gives" less lengthwise than crosswise. (A rare exception is hymo because the threads of its warp and woof are unlike, those of the warp being stretchier.) After you have made a few pairs of pants, your scrap box will supply silesia for many more.

Specify the length of the ZIPPER if you know it. If you don't yet know the correct length at the time you are ordering, just ask for "a pants zipper." Shortening one is a simple matter—I'll show you how when you get to that stage in the pants making.

A tailor's HOOK AND EYE are different from ordinary ones, which have sharp prongs to be forced through the waistband and bent flat on the back side. A tailor's hook is designed to take a length of linen tape, which distributes the strain over several inches of the waistband instead of in one pierced spot. At supply houses hooks and eyes are sold singly.

Be sure to say it is PANTS BUTTONS you want because they are the same size (24) as sleeve buttons but different from them in design. For flatness' sake the pants buttons have a groove between the holes for the thread to sink into.

LINEN TAPE is a great invention. It is a thin, white, smoothly woven tape, about ⅜ inch wide, of phenomenal strength. It is absolutely nonelastic and is used to stabilize all sorts of things: pocket openings, the bridle line of a coat, the entire outer edge of a well-made coat. In general sewing it is a guarantee against rips. Include it in any seams that take particular strain, such as tight waistlines or the armholes of children's clothes or sport clothes. A half-inch length of this tape, placed behind a seam and stitched in with it, will reinforce any *point* of strain; for example, the limits of pleats or of patch pocket stitching. A roll of it doesn't last very long at my house, but it can be bought by the yard.

The best LININGS for a man's coat are silk or Bemberg (rayon), 40 inches wide. Two and a half yards is enough for a full lining. Although ready-made coats are only half or quarter lined in the back, a custom tailor fully lines his coats, summer and winter. Besides being more luxurious, a fully lined coat is less prone to wrinkle across the back. A further advantage is that the seam allowances don't show through against the outside, because, not being exposed, they don't have to be booked (turned and hemmed). The tailors maintain that a fully lined coat is no warmer than a partially lined one, and the supply houses stock cool, porous lining fabrics for summer wear.

Hair canvas, or HYMO, is a highly resilient interfacing made of worsted, goat hair, and cotton. It is woven 66 inches wide, but the supply house will sell you a half width, which is enough for one coat. Hymo comes in a variety of weights, the best one being determined by the weight of the outer cloth. Its function in a coat is to reinforce the front and keep it permanently trim.

HAIRCLOTH is a wiry interfacing whose woof (crosswise threads, also known as "weft" or "filler") is hairs from the manes and tails of horses. It comes 16 to 20 inches wide and reinforces the shoulder area of the coat.

A layer of WHITE FELT encircles the armholes of a man's coat. This is a special tailor's felt, thinner than that sold in cloth stores.

The collar interfacing is cut from LINEN CANVAS, woven about 24 inches wide—a really nice canvas. Firm and heavily sized, it excels in taking and holding a smooth curve.

WIGAN (pronounced "wiggin") is a lightweight, plain-weave cotton fabric with little or no sizing. It is used to reinforce the fold at the bottom of the sleeve.

The undercollar is made of melton, a thick, heavily felted wool fabric that should be color matched to the outer cloth. Ask for an "UNDERCOLLAR CLOTH."

WADDING is very much like the cotton batting that goes into quilts, but thinner to make shoulder padding with imperceptible edges.

COAT BUTTONS are ordered as "one set, 3–6" or "3–4" or whatever you want. The first digit is the number of size-30 buttons for the coat front, and the second is the number of sleeve buttons.

MACHINE SILK THREAD is the very best kind for the construction of any wool garment. Unlike synthetic fibers, which stretch and recover, silk permanently molds with the cloth. This characteristic plus its small diameter make silk thread perfect for shaping and for almost invisible outside stitching. Buying it on the small spools in cloth stores can just about bankrupt you, so order a spool (800 yards!) from a supply house.

You need a spool of BUTTONHOLE TWIST, a soft silk thread of rather large diameter used for hand working buttonholes. Waxed, it also does a fair job of attaching buttons if you don't have button-and-carpet thread.

Although there is seldom a need to baste in general sewing, tailoring is often simplified by basting. Real BASTING THREAD is slick and strong and snarl resistant. It is also cheap, because it is made good by the addition of starch to a poor grade of cotton thread (which makes it unsuitable for permanent stitches in a washable garment). Because of its resistance to tangling, this thread can be handled easily in long strands; and, when it is time to remove the bastings, the strength and slickness allow you simply to loosen the last stitch and slip out the entire strand in one swoop. So do get the real thing. A 900-yard spool costs about half a dollar.

There are just two other small items, and I am sure you either have them already or can get them locally. The first is EMBROI-DERY FLOSS for the little thread marking you will do. Being fuzzy, it will cling to the cloth until you are ready to remove it. And the other item is a few scraps of UNBLEACHED MUSLIN, which you will use in the coat foundation.

CHAPTER 3

The Pants Pattern—from Scratch

Sure, you can buy a pants pattern, but there are two good reasons for making your own. The first is it's the only way you'll get a perfect fit. And the second is it will give you an insight into pattern alteration that no amount of theory can give you.

Pants patterns deservedly have a reputation of being difficult to alter. The problems arise because the seat section is at an angle to the leg, making any simple change in width affect the length as well, and vice versa. (See the illustration on the next page.)

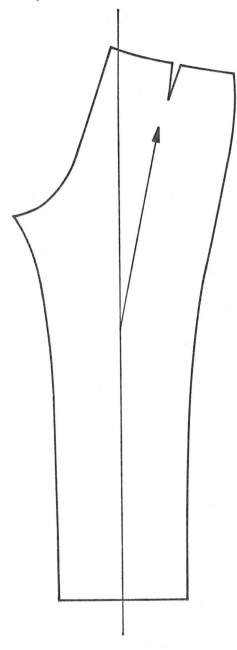

A pants back

An alteration in the length of the seat seam, for example, requires a change in the slope of the seat section if the width is to remain as is.

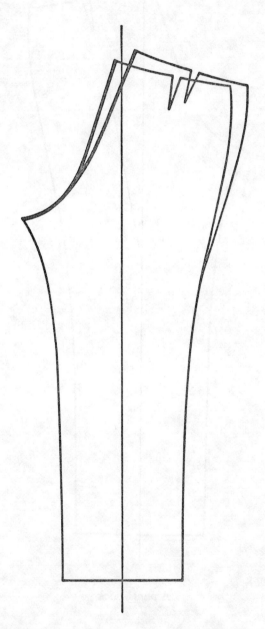

Lengthening (or shortening) the seat seam

In fact, the correct slope of the seat is dependent on three measurements: the waist, the seat circumference (hips), and the body height between the waist and seat. Change any one of these three dimensions, and you need a different slope for the pants back.

You can see why it is so hard to find ready-made pants that fit. The chance that a standard size will conform to any one person's waist *and* seat *and* vertical proportioning is small indeed.

In finished pants only slight alterations in width can be made satisfactorily. The pockets, and the fact that the waistband has no seam at the sides, make side seam alterations impractical—besides, there is no extra seam allowance there. So if pants are to be taken up or let out, it must be done in the center back seam.

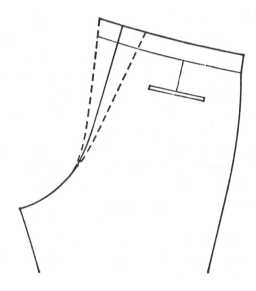

Changing the width at center back

Letting out in the center back sharpens the angle at the waist, while taking up blunts it. And that angle must be square if the waistband is to be horizontal in the back. I am sure you have seen waistbands that dip or go up to a point in the center back as a result of alteration.

Remember the "connect-the-dot" books you had when you were a child? The pages had a sprinkling of numbered dots. You found dot ✕1 and drew a line from it to ✕2 etc., and your lines gradually formed the outline of a picture. Well, that is how a pattern is drafted.

First you take certain measurements, and then working from them you locate and number various points on a big piece of paper. Then you connect points to form the outline of the pattern.

For a pants pattern you need six MEASUREMENTS:

Outseam	_____	
Inseam	_____	
Seat	_____	_____
Waist	_____	
Knee	_____	
Bottom	_____	

The measurements are taken with the man dressed normally in pants and shirt. Have him remove everything from his pockets and stand comfortably straight. For the OUTSEAM measurement ask him to adjust the *waistline* of his pants until it rests at the most comfortable height for him, no matter what that shifting does to the length of the pants or to their fit anywhere else. In line with the outseam (side seam) place the zero end of a tape measure at the waist edge of the pants (not at the waistline seam but all the way at the top edge of the pants), smooth it down along the outseam, and note the reading where it touches the floor. (See illustration on opposite page.)

Now it is time for him to decide how long he wants his pants. Adjust the bottom of a pants leg to the desired length and note its distance from the floor, taking care that the tape measure or ruler is vertical.

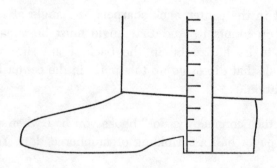

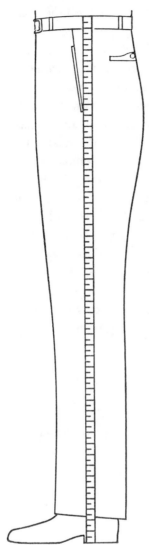

Measuring the outseam

The difference between these two readings is the outseam measurement. Record it.

For measurement of the INSEAM (the vertical seam on the inside of the pants leg) the belt should be removed. This time ask the man to adjust his pants to the height at which they are most comfortable through the *crotch and seat,* disregarding the height of the waistline. Place the zero end of the tape measure at the crotch (at the point where the inseams meet the seat seam), smooth the tape down along the inseam, and read the amount where it touches the floor. From this reading subtract the same amount you subtracted to get the outseam measurement, and record the result.

If you ever measure someone with whom you are not totally comfortable, reinforcing the first 6 inches or so of the tape measure with something like a thin wooden slat will make it easy to take the inseam measurement without embarrassment.

The outseam is what determines the length of the pants. When you lay the inseam measurement alongside it, what you are really deciding is how much height there will be between the waist and the crotch levels—in other words, how much the pants will *rise* from crotch to waist. This word RISE (or body rise) is the tailor's term for the difference between the lengths of the outseam and the inseam. (See illustration on opposite page.)

"Back rise" means the distance from the crotch to the waist as measured along the curved seat seam.

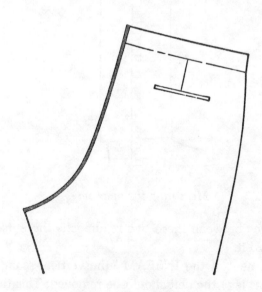

Back rise (heavy line)

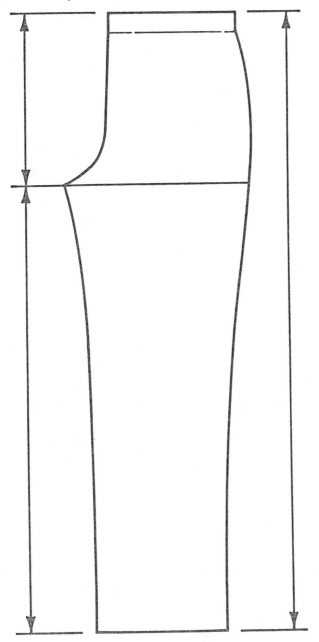

Rise equals outseam minus inseam

And "front rise" is the distance along the seam containing the fly.

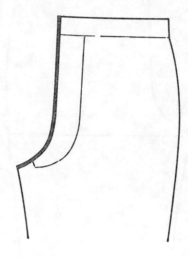

Front rise

If you want to compare the lengthwise proportioning of one pair of pants to another (perhaps to give yourself confidence in your measurements), compare the *difference* between the outseam and inseam (the body rise) instead of trying to measure along the curved back or front rise, which probably has stretched.

The SEAT measurement is taken horizontally around the fullest part of the buttocks. The tape should be fairly close but not tight—allowance for ease is added later. Some tailors pull the tape very tight and suddenly allow it to spring loose, taking the amount to which it springs to be the seat measurement. Others take it snugly and add 2 inches. I get good results holding a plastic tape measurement just tight enough that it won't slip down when held together in one spot. This is just an "easy" measurement—about the way a woman optimistically measures her own bust. Record whatever you decide on, and beside it write half the amount.

How tight does he want his pants at the WAIST? Most men insist upon having their waistbands too tight for the best appearance of the pants. The belt is what should take the strain, and the waistband should be just tight enough to be smooth. The easiest way to get an accurate waist measurement is to take it from a pair of pants that fit in the waist. Close the fasteners and stretch the waistband flat from the sides. Insert the zero end of a yardstick or 18-inch ruler at one side and read it at the other. Double the amount to get the full circumference. This method is more likely to be accurate than measuring around either a waistband or a man.

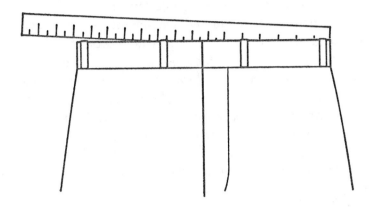

Taking the waist measurement from pants

The shape of the pants leg is a matter of style and personal preference. The KNEE and BOTTOM measurements are what you go by. They are most easily taken from a pair of pants with legs of the desired width and shape. Flatten a pants leg at the creases and measure across from crease to crease at the bottom and at the knee level (2 inches above the midpoint of the inseam). Double the readings to get the full circumference.

Now that you have taken the measurements, you need some big pieces of paper for drafting your pattern. The heavy brown wrapping paper used by many stores is ideal—the kind that comes 30 inches wide in big rolls. You need about 4 yards.

When you are ready to begin, lay out pencil, yardstick, tape measure, scissors, a drawing compass if you have one—a nonelastic string if you haven't, and something to help you draw right angles: drafting square, T-square, or just a perfectly rectangular piece of cardboard. Cut off a length of paper a foot or more longer than the outseam measurement and secure it to the work surface with sticky tape. Draw a straight line lengthwise in the middle of the paper, all the way from end to end. About 6 inches from the top, make a point on the line and label it "o."

The line is the grainline—the guide for positioning the pattern on the cloth. When you cut out the pants, you will lay this line parallel with the lengthwise threads. It is also the front crease line for the pants. And "o" is the starting point for locating the points to form the outline of the front piece of the pants pattern.

The instructions here are phrased like those in tailors' style books. My purpose is to make the trade jargon intelligible to you. When you know how to follow them, these books yield directions for drafting patterns for every conceivable tailored garment—dress clothes, riding breeches, clerical garb, vests, shirts, overcoats, service uniforms, women's suits and slacks—even a man's sheepskin coat. They are sold, however, only to members of the tailoring trade—or to persons believed to be in the tailoring trade! Publisher of some excellent style books, and of the weekly trade journal, *Tailor and Cutter,* is:

Tailor and Cutter, Ltd.
42 Gerrard Street
London, W. 1, England

In the illustration of the pants FRONT draft (next page) notice the lengthwise center line with the "o" near the top. In locating each of the points, first find it in the drawing so you know the direction in which to measure. The formal instructions are followed by any needed clarification.

1 from o is outseam less 1½ inches:

The point to be located is 1. Find it in the drawing (near the bottom of the lengthwise line). "From o" means you start measuring at o, and the distance is 1½ inches less than the outseam measurement. Mark the ⚹1 point on the paper, and label it "1" just as it is in the drawing.

2 from 1 is inseam:

Find 2 in the drawing. This time put the zero end of the tape measure on 1 and measure up along the line the length of the inseam. Label each point as you locate it.

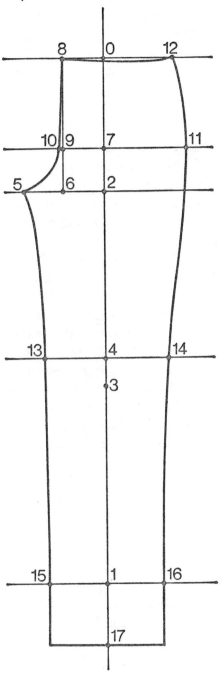

Pants front draft

3 is midway between 1 and 2
4 from 3 is 2 inches
Square out from 0, 2, 4, and 1:

Through those points draw crosswise lines at right angles to the lengthwise lines.

5 from 2 is ⅓ half-seat:

You remember I had you write down both the seat measurement and half of it—the "half-seat" measurement. In other pattern drafts you may find it called "the seat on the square" or just plain "scale." If you don't have a drafting square, divide the half-seat by 3 to get the distance of 5 from 2, locate 5 on the paper, and go on to the next formal instruction.

If you do have a tailor's drafting square, here is where you can begin to use it. On one side the square looks as if two pieces of yardstick, one longer than the other, had been put together to make a rigid "L." On the other side (the one that does the work) the arms are marked off in sections: 24ths, 12ths, 6ths, 3rds, and 2 thirds on the long arm; and 32nds, 16ths, 8ths, 4ths, and halves on the short one. Whenever a distance is given as a fraction of an amount (for example, "⅓ half-seat") find the appropriate section on the square (the 3rd section in this case) and then the amount (the half-seat measurement) within that section. From there to the zero end of the arm (the corner) is the distance you seek.

6 from 5 is ⅙ half-seat (midway between 5 and 2)
7 from 2 is ⅙ half-seat
Square out from 7
Square up from 6 to locate 8 on the line from 0, and 9 on the
    line from 7
10 from 9 is ¼ inch
Draw line 8–10
11 from 10 is ½ half-seat
12 from 8 is ¼ waist, plus ½ inch
13 from 4 is ¼ knee
14 from 4 is ¼ knee
15 from 1 is ¼ bottom
16 from 1 is ¼ bottom

17 from 1 (if no cuffs) is 2 inches, or
17 from 1 (if cuffs) is 3 times desired cuff depth, less ¼ inch
Square out from 17

You are ready to draw the outline of the front:

The waistline from 8 is squared by line 8–10 until it is about ¼ inch below line 8–12. Then it curves gently into 12.

The fly fall (front rise) follows the straight line 8–10 and then makes a shallow curve into 5.

Through 11 the outseam is vertical from about an inch above to a half-inch below. Continue upward, curving into 12 as shown in the illustration.

Shape the leg, making the inseam and outseam vertical from the bottom to at least 2 inches above 15 and 16 and identical to each other from the bottom to the knee. Above the knee the inseam is a natural continuation, waiting until almost the top to curve into 5. The outseam also continues naturally above 14, easing outward to meet the continuation downward from 11.

Cut out the pattern front. Seam allowances have been included, so the cutting line is the outline as you have drawn it. Cut notches as follows:

At points 0, 14, 16, 15, and 13.

In the outseam, 1½ inches below the waist edge, and again 6¼ inches below that (for the front pockets).

Front pocket notches

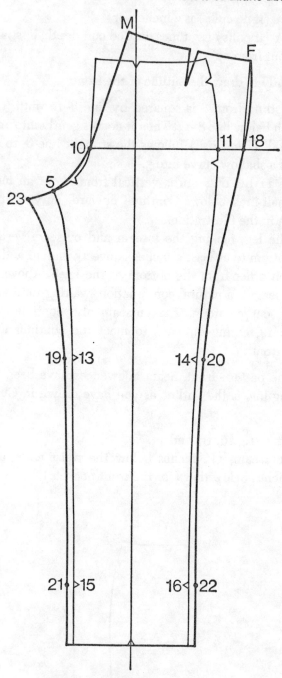

Pants back draft

In the fly fall about 1½ to 2½ inches from the inseam: Put the zero end of the tape measure ⅜ inch below the waist edge and measure along the fly fall ¼ inch in from the pattern outline. Cut the fly notch at the nearest whole inch, and that will be the length of your pants zipper.

Fly notch

For the pattern BACK tape another length of paper to the work surface and draw a line down the middle as you did before. Lay the pattern front on the paper, lining up the 0–1 line of the front with the line on the paper, and draw around it. Indicate notches and points 10 and 11. Take away the front and label points 5, 13, 14, 15, and 16. Draw line 10–11 and extend it to the right.

On a separate piece of paper, prepare to draft a PATTERN BACK GUIDE (page 38), which is my device for determining the slope of the back.

Draw the horizontal lines 0, 7, and 2 the same distance apart as on your pattern front. Near the right on line 2 give yourself a starting point, A.

B from A is ½ half-seat, plus 2 inches
Square up from A and B to locate C and D on line 0
E from B is ¼ waist, plus 1½ inches
F from C is ½ of E from A
G from D is ½ of E from A
Draw line A–F and locate X where it crosses the horizontal
  line 7

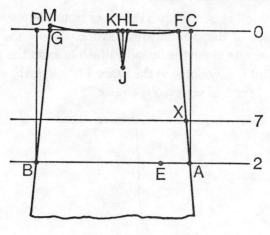

Pattern back guide

H from F is 4½ inches

From H square down 2½ inches to locate J

K and L are each ¼ inch from H

Draw lines J–K and J–L (back dart)

Draw line B–G and extend it ⅛ inch to M

From M square out to ⅛ inch below the horizontal line 0; then curve gradually into K

From L to F draw a curve that dips ⅛ inch below the straight line

Extend the straight lines M–B and F–A to several inches below line A–B, and cut out the pattern back guide, cutting along the curved lines M–K and L–F. Cut out the V for the back dart, all the way to J.

Going back to the big piece of paper and referring again to the illustration of the pants back draft,

18 from 11 is 2 inches

Place the X of the pattern back guide over point 18 on the paper. Using the common point as a pivot, swing the guide up until side M–B touches point 10 on the paper. And that is the correct slope for the seat.

Draw around the guide above 10 and 18 (X). Label M and F.

19 and 20 are ½ inch from 13 and 14

21 and 22 are ½ inch from 15 and 16

23 from 5 is $\frac{1}{12}$ half-seat (don't panic—it's half of 7 from 2), plus ⅜ inch:

If you have a compass, set it to the correct distance ($\frac{1}{12}$ half-seat, plus ⅜ inch), put the point of the compass on 5, and draw an arc in the vicinity of 23. If you don't have a compass, tie a non-elastic thread to the point of a pencil, and hold the thread against point 5 with your finger while you draw the arc.

23 from 19 is the same as 5 from 13:

Take the distance of 5 from 13, and measure it off from 19 to where it touches the arc. That point on the arc is 23.

And now the outline of the back:

The seat seam (back rise) follows the straight line M–10, becomes a shallow curve just outside the 10–5 curve of the front, and runs through 5 and into 23, finishing up straight for about the last inch.

From the bottom to the knee the inseam lies ½ inch outside the front outline. Above the knee it continues naturally, doing most of its curving into 23 near the top.

The outseam too is ½ inch outside the front outline from the bottom to just above the knee. Then it eases outward to pass through 18 and curve just outside the F–18 line into F.

The bottom is in line with that of the front.

Cut out the pattern back, and cut knee and bottom notches.

After you rest from that major accomplishment, let's look at what you've done.

It was rather like a map with lines of latitude and longitude. Do you see now why you alter the proportioning of a pattern *between* its strategic levels? You move the construction lines nearer or farther apart by folding out horizontally or by cutting the pattern apart and spreading the pieces. For example, in a dress or blouse, to raise or lower a bust dart, you want to move the bust *level* nearer or farther from the waist; merely redirecting the dart won't accomplish the purpose.

I told you the SEAM ALLOWANCE was taken care of, but maybe you'd like to know how. The tailor's standard seam allowance is ¼ inch. His way is to cut originally to the finished seam width and avoid trimming. Along any seam that may become involved in an alteration, such as the center back of pants, he allows enough to do some good; but this extra allowance is chalked onto the cloth just before cutting out—it does not appear on the pattern.

Vertically the only seam allowance you need is at the waist, because you have a turnup at the bottom. The 1½ inches you subtracted when you applied the outseam measurement represents the finished width of the waistband—still no seam allowance accounted for. But note that you measured vertically and then drew a curved outseam. The extra length of the curved line will be taken up as a seam at the waist and in making the bottoms slightly shorter in the front than the back, this latter being a refinement of custom-tailored pants.

Notice that all the seam allowance for the legs is added to the back piece of the pattern (½ inch each side—4 times ¼ inch). The body of the pants is wider in the back, and the greater width in the leg there makes the outseam and inseam less bias.

It was in locating point 18 that you incorporated both seam allowance and EASE (room to move) for the seat. Lines 10–11 on the front and 10–18 on the back together measure half the seat measurement, plus 2 inches. One inch represents 4 seam allowances, and the other is ease. Since the pattern covers half the body, that 1 inch for ease becomes 2 inches in the pants. If, after you complete your first pants, you conclude that a little more or less ease will improve the fit, make the change at point 18 and change by the same amount the distance of B from A in the pattern back guide, correcting the slope of the seat.

If you ever work from another pants draft, be wary of the way this seat slope is established. You may have to fall back on the method used here, because it is a matter in which the tailors are inclined to rely on their experience in preference to any formula. They study a man's profile and arbitrarily set the angle they hope will allow just enough room. When pressed for a rule, a tailor looks at what he has done and tries to figure some mathematical basis for it. Usually he hits upon a reference to the seat circumference, but

not always in the right direction. I am not exaggerating. Of approximately a dozen pants drafts that have appeared in trade pub-
lications over the past few years, about half claim rules that de-
crease the seat room for an increase in seat circumference! Some go
by such irrelevant data as the width of the pants leg, and one
author kindly indicates where the pattern should be subsequently
changed if the pants end up too large. Many talk of changing a
draft to accommodate "full seats" or "flat seats"—in other words, use
your own judgment. My search failed to turn up a single draft that
incorporated all three of the pertinent dimensions in setting the
slope of the seat. Well, after you have made a few hundred pairs
of pants for as many different men, you probably won't need a rule
either.

Only very tight pants need provision for DRESS. Ready-made
pants ignore it. The term refers to the side toward which a man
places the intimate parts of his anatomy when he puts on his pants.
A man is said to "dress right" or "dress left," and most men dress
left—a right dresser is sort of a southpaw to the tailoring trade.
Dress is allowed for by deflecting the fly seam away from the side
toward which the man dresses. The fork of one pants front, usually
the right, is reduced about ½ inch. If you make this provision, take
care not to hollow out too much or you will get a horizontal wrinkle
in the pants.

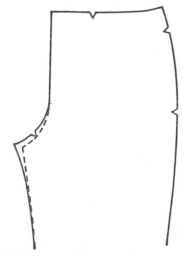

Provision for dress

If you go on to draft other pants patterns, there are at least a couple of ways you can speed the process. For the first time, I thought it simpler just to locate one point at a time without short-cuts. In the future, when measuring down from o to locate point ✳1, reverse the tape measure so points 1, 2, 3, and 4 can all be located without moving the tape. Similarly, points 5 and 6 can be located with one positioning of the tape or drafting square, as can the knee and bottom widths.

There are sources for patterns drafted to individual measurements. *Tailor and Cutter* offers such a service, and a supply house can always direct you to a tailor who provides patterns for a price. Custom patterns are expensive, however, and only the basic pieces are furnished—you are expected to cut your own auxiliary pieces, as you can now do for your pants pattern.

The FLY pattern conforms to the fly fall of the pants front. It is 2 inches wide, extends 1⅞ inches above the waist edge of the front, and ends ⅝ inch below the fly notch. Cut the fly notch, and another in line with the waist edge of the front.

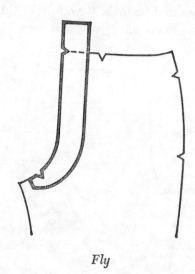

Fly

The FLY LINING is cut by the fly. At the top it is only as high as the upper notch of the fly, but it is 1½ inches longer and ¾ inch wider. Turn the piece to the back from the way it appears in the illustration, and write on it "right side up."

Fly lining

The CROTCH REINFORCEMENT matches the fork of the pants front. It extends from about 3½ inches above the crotch level to about 5 inches below it. Mark a grainline parallel with the inseam side.

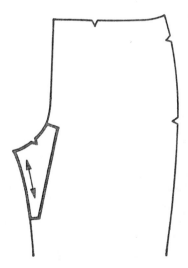

Crotch reinforcement

The FRONT POCKET is 13½ inches long. Draw the right side by the top and side of the pants front, but ½ inch below the lower pocket notch, jog outward ⅛ inch.

Cut around the right half of the pocket pattern, fold it 7 inches from the side, and draw around it for the left side. From the jog to the top, the left side is ½ inch wider than the right.

On the left side only, at the jog cut inward ⅛ inch. And on the right side at the top, do away with the corner, ¾ by ¾ inch.

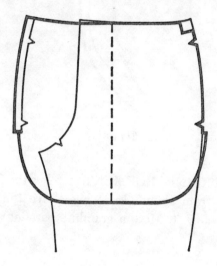

Front pocket

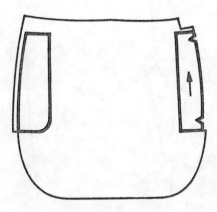

Front pocket facing and extension

The FRONT POCKET FACING and FRONT POCKET EX-
TENSION are cut by the pocket as shown. The facing (on the left
in the illustration page 44) is 2 to 2¼ inches wide, and the extension is about 1¾ inches wide. On the extension indicate which direction is up.

The pattern for the HIP POCKET TAB is 2⅝ inches long. In
width it is 1¼ inches at the top and 1⅝ inches at the widest level.

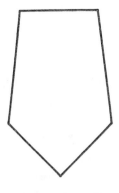

Hip pocket tab

The rest of the pants pieces are all rectangular and can be
chalked directly onto the cloth with a ruler. Their dimensions will
be given in the chapter on cutting out.

Somewhere on one of the big pieces of the pattern, record the date
and the measurements from which you worked. If you know the
man's weight, write that in too; then, if you return to the pattern
at some later date, a comparison with his current weight will indicate whether the pattern is still functional.

Roll the pattern pieces together instead of folding them. You will
be able to flatten them again by pressing with a warm, dry iron.

CHAPTER 4

Procedures and Preliminaries

One of the first skills a tailoring apprentice is taught is how to manage two layers of cloth in MACHINE STITCHING. He is given two equally long strips of soft wool and instructed to stitch them together without the aid of pins or basting and without allowing one to creep along the other. This is a knack that is easily acquired. The same principle of handling applies to almost all machine stitching (an exception is single knits), and it prevents both creeping and puckering.

If your sewing machine is in a cabinet, so you have a decent depth of counter between you and the needle, it *is* practical to sew long seams without pinning. If you are trying to sew on a portable machine without a cabinet, you may as well content yourself with pinning at least every 18 inches of a seam. After all, the idea is to simplify, not to add obstacles just to show you can overcome them. But proper handling does lessen the need for pins or basting.

Match the layers at the beginning of a seam and stitch the first inch or so paying no attention to alignment farther along. Then utilizing the full depth of your lead-in surface, match the top layer to the bottom so neither is stretched with respect to the other. At that distance pinch the layers together with your right hand, and with your left grasp the material where it has just emerged at the back of the needle. Holding the layers tightly together, stretch insistently and *equally* (so you don't interfere with the feed) with both hands while you stitch that portion of the seam.

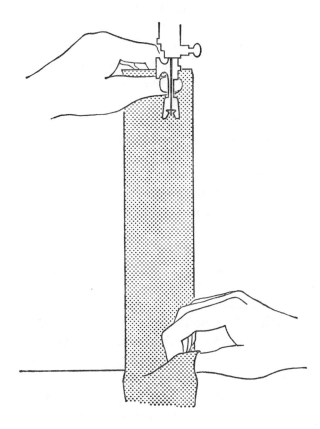

The material will go through the machine under tension, and upon release the thread will "relax" with the cloth, preventing puckering and insuring that the top layer melds to the bottom one as intended.

Repeat the process the length of the seam, working up to managing longer segments. At the end, a crosswise pin gives you something to hold to.

With firm cloth it is sometimes enough just to resist the flow with one hand. If you find that, to keep the layers from separating, you have to resist hard enough to interfere with the feed, then use both hands and pull equally. This approach will take you through even extreme situations, such as combinations of canvas and suiting, or seams that include pocketing, suiting, and linen tape. Whenever you join unlike fabrics, place on top the one less likely to stretch (as lining over wool) to minimize the tendency to creep.

The same method of control can be used to distribute ease, for example in a shoulder seam. In a well-drafted pattern a shoulder seam is about ½ inch longer on the back than the front. Pin the limits of the seam and stitch with the fuller (back) side down. Your stretching as you stitch will distribute the ease evenly.

It is more efficient to sew in short bursts, stopping to position the work a section at a time and then going at top speed, than it is to set a constant middle speed and chug along through varying degrees of control. A tailor at his power machine sounds like a swarm of furious hornets briefly silenced at intervals.

You may need a better understanding of the sewing MACHINE TENSION, especially if this is to be your first experience with silk thread. For that matter, to do any sewing at all you must be able to switch from one tension setting to another to adapt to different conditions of cloth or thread. There is no such thing as having the tension adjusted by a service man and that being that.

To adjust the machine tension for sufficient leeway for the variety of conditions you deal with, set the upper tension to about ⅓ its range (3 or 4 on a 10-point scale). Make sure there is no lint near the bobbin to distort the stitch. Thread the machine with your ordinary sewing thread, whatever you use most often for "plain" sewing, and test the stitch on two layers of medium-weight cloth, such as muslin. Leave the upper setting where it is, and adjust the *bobbin* tension until the stitch is even.

You should now be able to adapt to changes of cloth or thread by moving the upper tension setting only. Cloth that is harder to penetrate requires a higher setting; thread especially slick or fine (silk is in this category) and zigzag sewing call for a lower setting.

If you keep an eye on the quality of stitching the machine is turning out, you will become sensitive to shifts in the tension: After a while the stitch will pull to the bottom. What this means is that lint has collected around the bobbin and it is time to brush it out.

A common complaint having to do with machine tension is an unevenness of the stitch. You think you have the tension adjusted, only to have the stitch pull sometimes to the top and sometimes to the bottom, shifting capriciously of its own accord. This problem can almost always be traced to disuse of the machine. So long as a machine gets regular use, the continual passage of the thread keeps the tension-controlling grooves polished and smooth, and the tension is consistent. But when a machine sits idle, the moisture in the atmosphere attacks its metal surfaces, causing them to lose their polish. The obvious solution is to restore the polish. With the upper tension it is simple enough: Double a scrap of organdy, or similar highly sized or starched fabric, and work it back and forth between the tension plates.

With the bobbin tension it is not so simple, since you can't very well get at the inside grooves of the bobbin case. Insert a full bobbin, tighten the bobbin tension, and pull out the thread in long, steady pulls. If that doesn't suffice, try a long bout of steady stitching. A sewing machine needs occasional high-speed, prolonged stitching, in the same way a car requires a certain amount of highway driving, to stay in peak condition. If your home remedies fail to cure an unevenness of the stitch, replace the bobbin case with a new one. If you know ahead of time the machine is in for a long spell of idleness, you may be able to prevent bobbin tension trouble by storing the bobbin case (provided it is removable, of course) in a plastic bag containing silica gel, the chemical used for drying flowers.

Another machine problem you may encounter, especially with silk thread, is that sometimes thread tends to slide down the spool and tangle itself around the spindle. Some of the newer sewing machines prevent the problem by having the thread lead from the end of the spool. If your arrangement is the longtime standard one of having the thread unwind to the side, devise some way to cause it to lead upward as it leaves the spool. One way

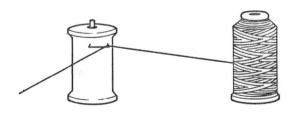

is to start from a lower spindle intended for bobbin winding. Another, if you have two spindles at the top of the machine, is to place on the left an empty spool with a staple or bent pin near the top, and then thread from the right.

While we are on the subject of the sewing machine, I want to suggest you add a guideline to your cabinet. DARTS are something that turn up in almost every garment you make. Their marking and stitching can be a breeze, or it can be very time consuming and even disastrous—I have seen a lot of beautiful cloth ruined with tracing carbon. I can't think of any excuse for owning a tracing wheel and carbon. If you will inscribe one line on your sewing machine cabinet, you will never again have to mark a dart at all. The line should be at right angles to the front edge of the cabinet and should lead directly toward the needle.

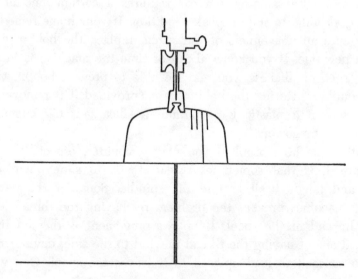

Guideline for stitching darts

When you cut out a pattern piece containing a dart, indicate the point with a pin, and in the seam allowance cut a notch at each side of the dart.

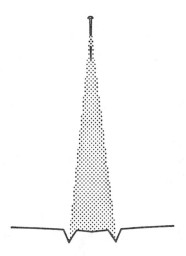

Marking a dart with pin and notches

When you fold the dart for stitching, match the notches. Start stitching at the point of the dart with the notches on the guideline on the cabinet. For a straight dart, you have only to guide the notches along the line. For a curved dart, with the point and end so marked, you should be able to complete the line by referring to the pattern piece as you stitch.

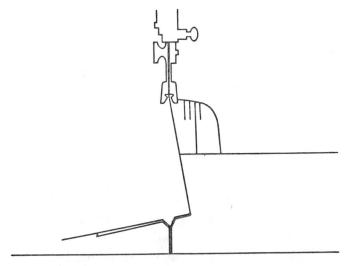

Stitching a dart

I like one-thread darts. They leave no dangling thread ends and no extra thickness from backstitching to distort the point of a dart. You can make them on any standard sewing machine: With the machine threaded normally, pull up about 18 inches of thread from the bobbin (more or less, depending on the length of the dart). Unthread the machine needle and leave the upper thread dangling. With the bobbin thread, rethread the needle *backward.* Lay the thread ends together and join them in a tight, single-loop knot. Lift the spool from the spindle while you wind up the slack thread. The knot will pass through the tension plates and end up near or on the spool.

The machine now has a single continuous thread from bobbin to top. Start the dart stitching at the point with the first stitch as close to the fold as you can get it. At the end you can still backstitch for security. Of course the process has to be repeated for each dart. Let the knots collect on the spool until you have stitched the last dart. Then unthread the needle and pull off all the knots at once.

PRESHRINKING is such a simple precaution that to omit it is foolish, especially when the consequence can be so disheartening. A tailor preshrinks as a matter of course—everything from the most expensive suiting (whether or not a label disclaims the necessity) to the cheapest cotton canvas.

The word itself is a misnomer. Thoroughly shrinking suiting would destroy its workability. The aim rather is to *condition* the cloth to go through the cleaning process without either shrinking or stretching. Whenever you are in doubt as to what constitutes adequate preshrinking, subject the cloth to a normal cleaning before cutting into it to insure that it is preshrunk.

Steam pressing with a household iron effactually preshrinks only thin materials, such as silk or Bemberg. Canvases (including hymo and haircloth) must be thoroughly wet, partially dried, and ironed dry—preferably with a tailor's iron. Pocketing and sateen are borderline: When they go into a garment destined for dry cleaning, steam pressing is probably a sufficient precaution (at least I have never gotten into trouble that way); but, for a washable garment, pocketing and sateen should be preshrunk in the same way as canvas. Felt, wadding, and undercollar cloths need no pretreat-ment (I assume they won't be subjected to washing). Neither do the wigan and muslin for a man's coat, because they are used in the form of bias strips.

The easiest way to preshrink suiting is to take it to a dry cleaner and have him do it. If you do very much of it yourself, you will want a board about 32 inches long and 9 to 12 inches wide, shellacked to make it impervious to moisture. You also need an old bed sheet split in half lengthwise. Leave the suiting folded once lengthwise (the way it comes); wet and wring the sheet. Lay one end of the double-thickness suiting on your pants board or kitchen counter. Place a single thickness of damp sheet over it; put the board on top; and fold toward you (board, sheet, and suiting) until the entire length is wound smoothly onto the board. Weight it with the coat board, and leave it for a couple of hours. Then spread the suiting flat to dry, and lightly steam press on the back side.

PRESSING is an adventure when you have a tailor's iron. As-semble the pants board, coat/sleeve board, press cloth, iron, a bowl of water, and a sponge.

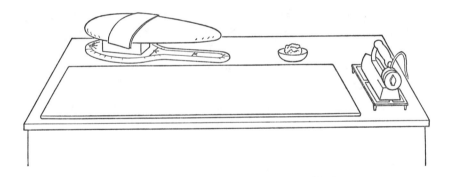

Set the iron control to "high." Because of its huge mass a tailor's iron is slow to heat. You want it just hot enough to sizzle smartly when you test it with a moist finger—about like a high wool setting on a household iron. As soon as it gets up to temperature, turn it to "low." At that setting a tailor's iron is designed to hold press-ing temperature safely for hours.

Some practice with wool scraps will make pressing a more relaxed part of pants making. First, try making creases. Fold a scrap right side out and lay it on the pants board. Lay the press cloth, rough side down, over the scrap to avoid the shine that would be imparted to wool by direct contact with the iron. With the sponge, dampen the press cloth where it lies over the proposed crease.

The iron is too heavy for you to be able just to reach out and pick it up comfortably. Stand squarely with your feet slightly apart. Make sure the cloth is in complete readiness and that you know exactly where you want to put the iron. Reach out with a swaying motion of your whole body, grasp the iron, and on the return swing of your body bring the iron with you and deposit it where you planned. You should hear a moderate sizzle from the press cloth. Rotate the iron a bit and move it farther along the crease. Before the moisture is quite used up, return the iron to its stand, quickly raise the press cloth, and allow the wool to finish steaming undisturbed. Don't rush it—damp wool is vulnerable to stretching.

When the iron is placed against the damp press cloth, it clings at first. As the moisture dries out, there is a point at which the iron turns loose easily. If it tends to stick, one of three things is probably at fault: residual sizing in the press cloth, too high a temperature, or too low a temperature. But that is why you are experimenting: to learn how hot, and how long, is enough.

When you are able to make sharp, durable creases, move on to practice pressing ¼-inch seams open. First press the seam unopened (as it was stitched) without moisture, to smooth any tendency to pucker. Since in this step you are using a dry iron directly against the suiting, it is a good habit to touch the iron first to the cool press board as a precaution against its being too hot. Then lay the scrap opened, seam side up, on the board. Dip your fingertips into the bowl of water and run them along the inside of the seam. In pressing open a seam, you don't need to use a press cloth unless the seam contains alteration allowance that might someday be on the outside of the garment.

As you press, watch for a tendency of the seam to leave an impression against the outside of the cloth. It may be that your pants board lacks firmness and is letting the seam sink into it. If the tendency is slight, you can overcome it by laying heavy paper under each side of the seam when you press. Or the indentation can be removed by a second pressing from the outside, this time with a press cloth of course.

Remember, the first criterion of good tailoring is flat seams. Pressing each seam as you go, sometimes even from both sides, flattens most effectively. Thorough pressing is especially important when several seams end up on top of each other, for example in pockets.

Do some experimenting. Nobody can tell you in advance exactly how your cloth will behave in pressing—just what combination of heat, moisture, and exposure time it will respond to best. Start out conservatively: that is, using plenty of moisture and not too much heat and exposure. If the results are not satisfying, make gradual adjustments until you find the optimum set of conditions.

Be deliberate in your motions, and facility will come. You have to realize that you can't stand and hold the iron while you arrange your work. Anytime the iron is in the air, it should be in motion—a swinging motion well aimed to take it from where it was resting to where it is to rest. Getting a tailor's iron into position takes a little effort, but, once it's there, the iron's weight does all the work.

CHAPTER 5

Cutting Out the Pants

If I had you here personally and could teach you just one thing, it would be how to manage shears. Nothing so quickly reveals the degree of one's sewing ability as the way he cuts out, and the person who cuts out well is as rare as is an expert in any other skill.

I have seen people (including teachers of custom dressmaking) cut out sloppily and then spend hours marking the seam line with chalk or tracing paper. The first rule of cutting is *cut accurately*. Then you have no need to mark seam lines; you can confidently guide the stitching by the cut edge.

In case you skipped over the reference to accuracy, pause to consider the effect of a habitual ⅛-inch discrepancy. Many people in cutting out have a fear of cutting too close, so they go along about ⅛ inch outside where they ought to be. (The practice is so common that one pattern company attempts to avert trouble by printing a double cutting line with instructions to cut midway between.) When these people go to a machine, they tend to stitch ½-inch seams instead of the standard ⅝. In just four seams that much difference amounts to 2 full inches, or a *full size change* in a four-piece skirt. When you lay out the pattern pieces for pants, you will chalk the outline onto the cloth. In cutting out, aim to split the chalk line.

Cut all the way to the tips of the shears every time, or you'll soon find it impossible to do so. Stopping shy wears a burr on the cutting edge, and ever afterward the shears balk at that point. If you have only a tiny cut to make, do it with the tips of the shears. Use most of the blade length as often as you can, starting the cut with the blades not quite all the way open. Never jam the shears into the cloth; close the blades together in it. Hold the shears perpendicular to the cutting board (not leaning to either side), and pull back ever so slightly as you cut. What that does is keep the layers of cloth from separating, so they both get cut identically. It takes practice to exert just enough resistance that both layers of cloth are under control and yet the blades don't slip backward. Once you have this knack of holding back as you cut, you won't waste time pinning elaborately. Two pins will keep a pattern piece of tissue paper from blowing off position, and a weight or two will anchor heavier patterns.

New shears must be broken in, and even badly misused ones can be considerably improved the same way: Run the spout of a can of machine oil along the cutting edges, depositing a thin coat of oil. Also place a drop at the screw. Slowly open and close the shears several times. Wipe the oil from them, and cut through a scrap of cloth until no trace of oil remains. Whenever shears start to pull in cutting (and it will be often with new ones), stop and oil the blades. As you cut out, periodically wipe the lint from the blades with your fingertips or a cloth, and be sure the shears are completely closed before they are laid down. If you oil shears frequently in the beginning, you will soon be able to neglect them. Mine have had fifteen years of hard use with very little pampering since their careful break-in period, and they still don't need sharpening.

Another good cutting habit pertains to the smaller trimmers: Trimming with the blunt-ended blade down lessens the risk of snagging something.

You have some further choice about the styling of your pants. Two decisions should be made before you cut out.

For one thing, there has been a revival of interest in pocket watches. If you would like to have a WATCH POCKET in your pants, cut those pieces that pertain to one; if not, omit them.

For another, you may or may not want PLEATS. To adapt the pattern for pleats, cut along the grainline of the pattern front from the waist to the knee, and spread the sides for the depth pleat you want. In the cloth, extend the waist cut across the pattern separation, and give yourself a notch at each side.

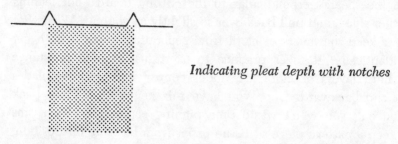

Indicating pleat depth with notches

It has long been customary in the United States for pants pleats to turn outward, though there is some trend toward copying the

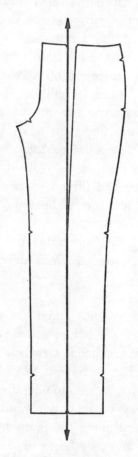

American-style pleats

European style, which is the reverse. For American-style pleats, observe the grainline of the front portion of the pattern. And for European pleats, cut the side portion on the straight. (See page 58 and below.)

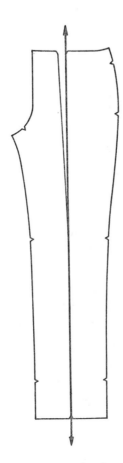

European-style pleats

Believe it or not, you are ready to cut out. Lay out the OUTER CLOTH folded lengthwise with the selvages carefully matched. Anytime you cut out in double thickness, have the *right sides together*. That way the back of the cloth is outermost for marking, and pieces that will be sewn together as cut are already right sides together for stitching.

These are the pieces to be cut from the outer cloth:

> 2 fronts
> 2 backs
> 2 flies
> 1 upper fly facing (2½ by 2½ inches)
> *2 front pocket facings
> *2 front pocket extensions
> *4 hip pocket facings (7⅛ by 2⅛ inches)
> 2 hip pocket tabs
> *2 waistbands (in length, ½ the waist measure, plus 4 inches, and in width 2¼ inches) See warning below
> 2 belt loop strips (12 by 1⅛ inches)
> *2 watch pocket facings (one 4 by 2½ inches and the other 4 by 2 inches)

Warning: If the selvages are wider than ⅜ inch, the waistbands must be cut wider by whatever amount the selvages exceed ⅜ inch.

In men's suitings the selvages are woven to be used; they are the thinnest, neatest seam finish you can have. In the preceding list, the pieces marked with asterisks (*) are best cut on the selvages. If you don't have enough selvage length, transfer first the watch pocket facings and then the front pocket *extensions* to the body of the cloth, and later overcast the edges to simulate a selvage.

The arrangement of the pattern pieces of course depends on their size and the width of the cloth. The illustration on page 61 is a possible layout in 1½ yards of 60-inch suiting. Note that here the watch pocket facings have been crowded off the selvages.

Many solid color cloths have a nap (an up and a down) too slight to be discerned by superficial looking and feeling, but pronounced enough to show up in a finished garment. The only way to rule out nap with certainty is to join two scraps cut in opposite directions, press the seam open, and study the sample in daylight. If you are sure the cloth has no nap, you may be able to place the pattern pieces to better advantage by reversing the direction of either the front or the back.

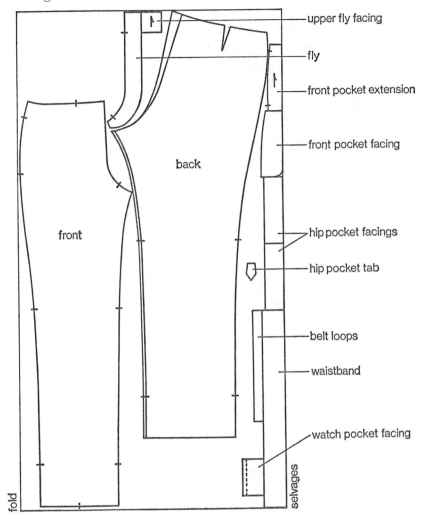

upper fly facing

fly

front pocket extension

front pocket facing

back

hip pocket facings

hip pocket tab

front

belt loops

waistband

watch pocket facing

selvages

fold

Cutting layout for pants

Another acceptable compromise is to throw the back (but never the front) slightly off the grainline. And in a real pinch, you can piece the fork of the back: Make the separation in line with the lengthwise threads. Later, add a scrap in a ¼-inch overcast seam, and trim to the pattern shape. (See illustration page 62.)

In slacks for a large man, a tailor often resorts to piecing the fork. In an entire suit, there is little excuse for this expedient, because pants and coat pieces can be cut alongside each other without waste. Several pairs of pants also can be cut from the same cloth with little waste. For this reason, a pieced fork in ready-made pants suggests perhaps too much corner cutting by the manufacturer.

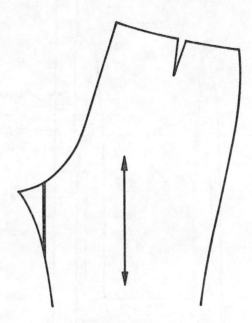

Piecing the back fork

When you have the pattern pieces arranged to your satisfaction, secure them with weights (whatever is handy—I use wooden drink coasters; a friend of mine uses bean bags), and chalk the pattern outlines onto the cloth. Work with an entire side edge of the chalk flat against the cloth so you don't wear down the corners unevenly. When the chalk gets dull, sharpen it (if wax) by scraping with a knife or (if clay) by rubbing the chalk on fine sandpaper against a flat surface.

There are two places where you need to make allowance for possible alterations: at the seat seam, tapering from nothing to about 1 to 1½ inches at the waist (consult the illustration of the pattern layout), and the length of the back inseam (chalk a second line ½ inch outside the first). At the inseam it is only near the top that you are likely to need the allowance, but a full-length, even addition makes thread marking unnecessary.

At each notch, chalk a short crosswise line to remind you to cut the notches outward. Be sure to indicate the knee and bottom notches on the outer (cutting) line of the back inseam. If you are working with wax chalk on wool, you know you can erase an imperfect line with a warm iron and try again. If you are using clay chalk, mark lightly—it is hard to erase short of dry cleaning or washing, though a good brushing helps.

If there can be any confusion of right and wrong sides of the cloth, lightly chalk a mark to identify the back side of each piece as soon as it is cut out. On the upper fly facing and the front pocket extensions, mark a half-arrow to indicate "up."

The only place you need to thread mark (tailor tack) is the seat seam. With two strands of embroidery floss in a color contrasting with the cloth, make a coarse running stitch along the inner chalk line through both thicknesses, leaving quite a bit of slack between stitches. Clip the thread midway between the stitches; gently separate the layers of cloth; and again cut the thread midway between the layers so half the thread remains in each layer.

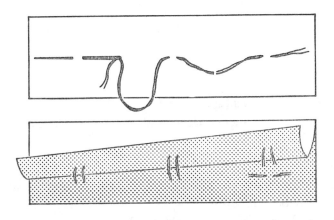

Thread marking

From the POCKETING cut:

> 2 front pockets
> 2 hip pockets (7½ by 16½ inches)
> 1 watch pocket (5½ by 4 inches)

On the wider side of the front pockets, cut inward ⅛ inch at the jog, just as you did on the pattern piece.

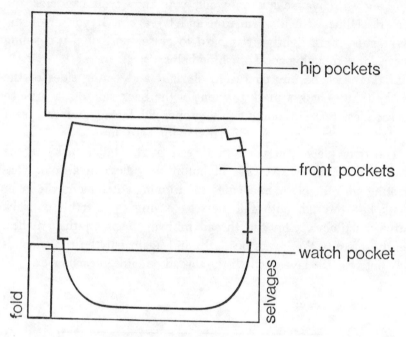

Pocketing layout

From the SATEEN cut:

> 2 waistband linings (same as your waistband)
> 2 curtains (3½ inches deep and 1½ inches longer than the waistband)
> 1 fly lining

These pieces you can pink if you have pinking shears. The fly lining can be cut either lengthwise or crosswise, but be sure you get it right side up (the back side is uppermost in the illustration).

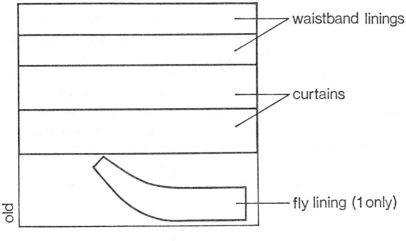

Sateen layout

From the SILESIA cut:

   2 facings for upper edges of hip pockets (1 by 7 inches)
   2 crotch reinforcements
   1 fly interfacing (by fly pattern, but at the top only as long
     as the upper notch)

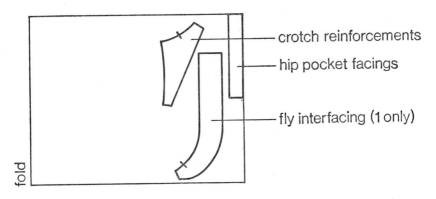

Silesia layout

    The facings don't have to be on the selvages, but if you have a place for them there you might as well use it. If you have pinking shears, pink the long side of each crotch reinforcement.

    Pants made of good suiting do not need to be lined, but those of scratchy cloth or cloth that doesn't hold a crease well are improved by lining. You sometimes see pants that have a patch of lining material inside the knee. Such a patch may make the pants a little more comfortable for kneeling, if that is what they are designed for, but it does absolutely nothing to prevent stretching of the pants knee. If you line at all, line at least the entire front. The way to do it is to *underline;* that is, cut out a whole pants front of lining material, place it against the outer cloth, and treat the two as one piece of cloth all the way through the construction. For the lining material, choose the softer rayon sheath lining in preference to taffeta-like fabric so the wearer won't swish when he walks.

CHAPTER 6

Making Up the Pants

The first step in making up pants is to OVERCAST the lengthwise edges of the fronts and backs (outseams, inseams, and rise) as a seam finish. Mercerized cotton or cotton/polyester thread, not silk, is best for overcasting. I use the widest plain zigzag stitch on my machine at about 10 stitches per inch.

If your machine won't zigzag, you have no choice but to overcast by hand, using two strands of thread. Comfort yourself that many of the old-time tailors still do it that way.

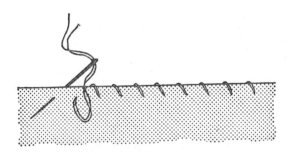

Overcasting by hand

And the second step, strangely enough, is to press in the FRONT CREASES with finality: from the bottom to the crotch level if the pants are pleatless, all the way to the top if they are to have pleats. Use the waistline notch to help locate the crease on the grainline.

If you are making PLEATS, proceed to stitch them now: Match the notches, right sides together, and stitch within the crease a length of 1½ inches. From that point, turn and stitch downward in a 45-degree angle to the fold. Turn again and stitch on the fold back up to the waist.

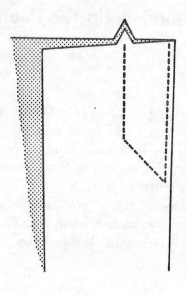

Stitching a pleat

On the back side, turn each pleat toward the front for American style, or toward the side for European, and anchor it by stitching ⅛ inch from the waistline edge.

The pants board is a perfect non-slip surface for aligning pieces. Lay out the FRONT POCKETS right side up. Place the pants fronts right side up over the pockets, matching notches at the outseam. Lay the front pocket extensions right side down over the fronts, again matching notches. On each pocket extension, baste a length of linen tape ¼ inch from the outseam edge, through all thicknesses. On the outer edge of the tape, stitch from notch to notch, leaving long thread ends for easy tying. (Illustration page 69.)

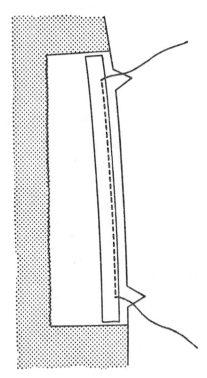

First seam of the front pocket

To secure each end of the stitching, pull one thread through so both are on the same side, and tie a square knot: Loop the right strand over and through the left—

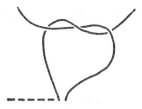

Square knot begun

Pull the threads tight; loop the left over and through the right, and pull again.

Rather than leave the threads going in opposite directions and in danger of working loose, smooth them together as one and tie a tailor's knot (also known as a weaver's knot): Make a single large loop—

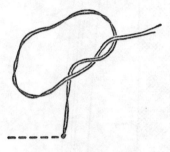

Tailor's knot begun

You can slip the knot in either direction depending on which side of the loop you pull. Slip it down onto the square knot—

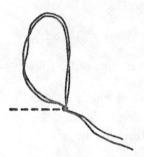

Tailor's knot ready to be pulled tight

And place a finger lightly over the knot while you pull the threads tight.

Usually threads can be fastened by backstitching at the beginning and end of a seam, but in this pocket seam you don't want any extra thickness at the ends to distort the graceful curve, and you want the last stitches clearly differentiated for precise ends to the pocket opening.

At each of the pocket notches, cut inward (all thicknesses) to the last stitch. Remove the bastings and press the seam open on the coat board. Be sure the seam really is open underneath too, with the front going one way and the extension the other.

Turn the extension to the underside, encouraging the seam just out of sight, and baste a little more than ¼ inch from the fold. Topstitch, notch to notch, at ¼ inch. Remove bastings, and press to flatten.

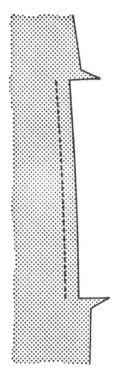

Topstitching, front pocket

Stitch the selvage of the extension to the pocket. Place a front pocket facing across from the extension ⅜ inch in from the side of the pocket (as in the illustration that helped you cut the facing and extension patterns on page 44). Join the facing to the pocket by stitching on the selvage and part way around the bottom.

Close the pocket with a french seam in this way: Fold the pocket lengthwise with the facing and extension on the outside.

Take a ⅛-inch seam from the jog, down around the curve, and over to the fold.

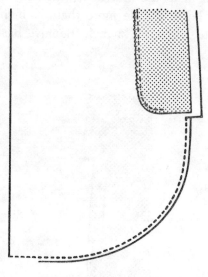

Closing the front pocket

Turn the pocket right side out and stitch that same seam a second time, this time at ¼ inch. On the front side of the pocket just above the french seam, cut inward ½ inch (¼ inch beyond the seam).

Clip at upper end of french seam

With the pants front right side up, line up the outseam above the pocket with the pocket facing underneath, and press in the pocket fold. Fold the back of the pocket (pocketing only) out of the way, and stitch crosswise at each end of the topstitching:

Just stitch two or three times and clip the thread ends close. These spots will be restitched later, adding in another thickness.

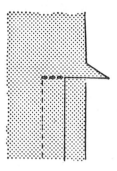

Topstitching (upper) end of pocket opening

The fronts are now ready for the outseams. Before you go to the backs, I want to prevent a common fitting fault, whose solution may be unexpected.

The back dart lines on patterns for both men and women are straight lines, but the majority of people have at least some hollowing in the small of the back. Stitching the darts straight leaves slack in the garment, resulting in a horizontal wrinkle at center back just below the waistband. Because the wrinkle is horizontal, the tendency is to try to remove it by setting the waistband lower in the back. But that spoils the hang of the garment, as can be seen best in an exaggerated side view of a straight skirt.

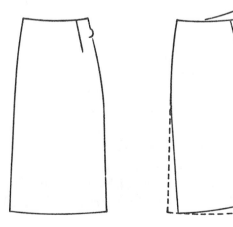

Instead, the solution is to shape the back darts. With the machine needle set into the point of the dart, and the notches on the machine guideline ready for stitching a straight dart, force a curve into the cloth between needle and notches. Stitch "straight," and when the cloth relaxes you will have stitched a curve.

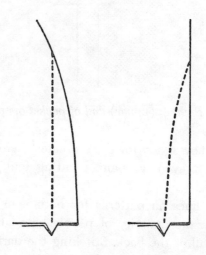

Shaping a dart

An almost imperceptible curving of the dart can work wonders. Because the change is multiplied by the two sides of the dart and again by the number of darts, a ⅛-inch curve, for example, in just two darts pinches out ½ inch of cloth across the back. If necessary, in the pants you can also shape the crotch seam at center back.

Stitch the DARTS in the backs: Begin ½ inch below the V-cut, and stitch to ¼-inch seam width at the waist. Press the seams open.

On the outside of the backs, chalk the position of each HIP POCKET: You want a 6-inch straight line parallel to the waist, at the level of the dart's point and centered with it. Indicate the limits of the line with short vertical marks.

Place a hip pocket right side up, selvage end down, underneath each pants back with the upper (raw) end of the pocket ¾ inch higher than the chalk line on the back and centered crosswise with it. (Crease the pocket end to find the middle, and match it to the dart.) Baste the two together along the chalk line.

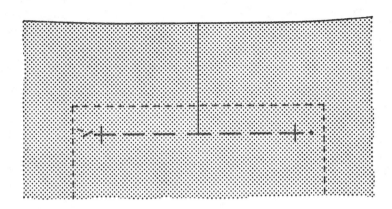

With the pants back still right side up, lay an upper edge facing (silesia) face down above the basting line with its lower (raw) side touching the line. Stitch through all three thicknesses ⅛ inch above the line, observing its limits.

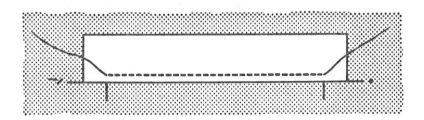

Lay a hip pocket facing (outer cloth) right side down with its upper (raw) side touching the line of *stitching*. Over it baste a length of linen tape ¼ inch below the raw edge of the facing. Stitch on the upper edge of the tape, making the limits correspond with those of the first stitching.

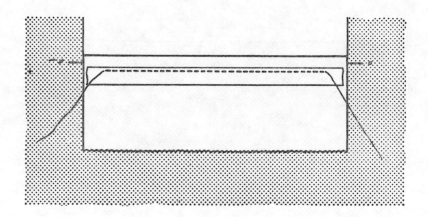

Examine the back side to verify that the two lines of stitching are parallel and a good ¼ inch apart. (Tailors speak of a "good" or a "scant" amount, meaning 1⁄16 inch more, or less. A "good ¼ inch" then is midway between ¼ and ⅜, and a "scant ¼ inch" or "good ⅛ inch" is midway between ¼ and ⅛.) Pull the threads through to the back side and tie knots.

Two tips for ending a line of stitching exactly on a point: If you need less than a whole stitch, leave the presser foot down so you don't disturb the alignment of the various layers, lower the needle until it almost touches the cloth, and move the stitch length lever until the needle will enter where you want it. If you remove the work from the machine and *then* discover one line is too short, use a hand sewing needle to pass the outer thread through at the correct point, and tie the thread ends.

Remove both bastings, and press *open* the lower seam (the upper part of the back folds down at the seam, and the facing and its seam allowance are up).

You will now form a piping for the lower edge of the pocket: Fold the facing snugly over its seam allowance and the linen tape, and baste beneath the seam. From the right side, stitch within the seam, including the facing underneath.

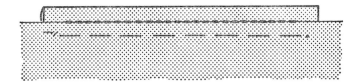

Remove the basting and cut the pocket open: Hold the facing out of the way and cut through the pants back and the pocketing, midway between the two lines of stitching. Half an inch from the ends, begin curving toward the last stitches and cut right up to them, but don't cut the thread!

With the facings still on the front side, pull the upper one down firmly over its seam allowance and stitch on it ⅟₁₆ inch from the seam. This second stitching is to make the seam tuck out of sight when you turn the facing to the underside. Do so now, and baste at about ¼ inch, making the line of basting no longer than the seam. Push the lower facing also through to the inside.

Stitch the ends of the pocket opening: With the pants back right side up, fold back the side of the pants and the pocketing to expose the facings and the little triangles of cloth that were formed when you cut open the pocket. Stitch back and forth between the last stitches of the two seams.

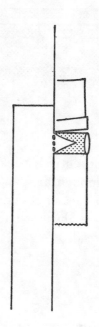

Each pocket facing of outer cloth should be narrower than the pocketing by a good ⅛ inch at each side. If it isn't, trim it. Fold up the pocket so its dangling (selvage) end is even with the waist edge of the pants back (even at the sides—the center will be a little higher because of the curve of the waist). Indicate the fold by nicking each side of the pocket no deeper than 1/16 inch.

Fold down the selvage end of the pocket in line with the pocket opening, and crease it with your fingernail. Open down the pocket.

Place a hip pocket facing, right side up and selvage up, across the pocket so the lower (raw) side is ½ inch down over the crease.

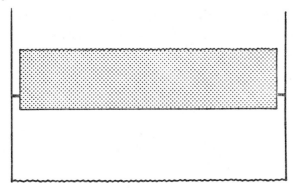

Stitch the selvages of both facings to the pocket.

Fold up the pocket at the nicks with the facings on the outside, and stitch the sides in ⅛-inch seams. Turn it right side out and stitch again at ¼ inch, tapering the upper end by folding in the sides.

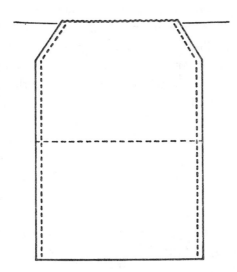

Stitch around the two pieces of the POCKET TAB right sides together, in a ⅛-inch seam, leaving the top open. At the point, take one shorter stitch straight across, so you turn on two stitches instead of one (a good practice anytime you have an angle sharper than a right angle).

Press the seam open (over a pencil), turn the tab right side out, and baste about ¼ inch from the edge. Press, remove basting, and press again.

Do you want to make your BUTTONHOLES by machine or by hand? There are only two in the pants, one on the tab that shows, of course, and one at the waist that does not. I work a buttonhole first by machine with cotton or cotton/polyester thread, using a keyhole cam in my buttonhole attachment (a valuable attachment even for a zigzag machine). The machine stitches make an outline that is easy to follow, and form a filler, or padding, for the hand stitches. The finished buttonhole gives the appearance of being completely hand worked. This way is much simpler than the tailor's, which is to begin with a cut and to work over a filler of two strands of buttonhole twist. If you have a buttonhole attachment with a standard set of cams, you will see there are two, ⅝ and 1¹⁄₁₆ inches, that make a buttonhole with one rounded end (keyhole). The ⅝ inch is the right size for pants buttons.

At this stage on the pants, do whatever machine work you intend for the buttonhole on the pocket tab. Hand working instructions follow in the finishing stages of the pants. Place the upper ½ inch of the pocket tab, centered, under the upper edge of the left hip pocket opening, and pin.

From the right side, through all thicknesses, stitch the ends and the upper edge of each hip pocket opening: within the seams at the ends (back and forth several times) and ¹⁄₁₆ inch above the upper edge. Pull tightly and evenly as you stitch so the layers don't creep. Remove the basting and press.

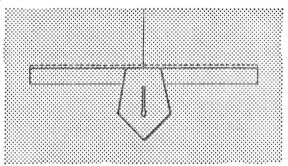

Stitch the OUTSEAMS at a good ¼ inch: Use a zipper presser foot so you can stitch right up against the front pocket openings, and again exclude the backs of the front pockets. Press the seams open.

Baste each CROTCH REINFORCEMENT in place against the inside of the front at the fork—a simple instruction, but this is a good place to introduce tailor's basting:

For general purposes there are two kinds of basting, each useful

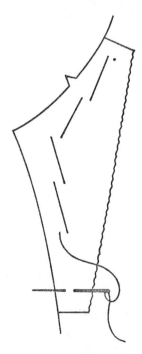

Basting the crotch reinforcement

in its place: a running stitch, which stabilizes in only one direction, and tailor's basting, which holds both ways and is an extremely fast way to cover territory. Tailor's basting is just a series of stitches at right angles to the direction you are going. It shows up as diagonals on the working side.

Place the LEFT FLY against the left pants front, right sides together and fly notches matched. Put the fly interfacing over the fly, notches matched. Take a ¼-inch seam, beginning at the fly notch and stopping ¾ inch below the waist edge.

Turn the fly (the interfacing will come with it) firmly out toward the front, over the seam allowance, and from the outside stitch on the fly about $\frac{1}{16}$ inch from the first seam. This is the same "tucking" seam you made on the upper edge of the hip pockets.

Overcast together the raw side and end of the fly and interfacing as a seam finish.

Before you stitch the BELT LOOP strips, you need to decide how you will turn them right side out. This is another case where you can make a better tool than you can buy, this time by bending and filing a hook at one end of about an 18-inch length of coat hanger wire.

Belt loop turner

In spite of the fact that it rusts and so must be rubbed with a rag before each use, this tool is much better than the dainty, fragile belt loop turners sold at notions counters. To use it, insert it into a strip, snag the far end, and pull.

You can turn strips without hardware: Trim one end to a sharp point before stitching, attach the end of a string to the back side of the point, and fold point and string against the right side of the strip so you enclose the string when you stitch. To turn the strip right side out, pull the string.

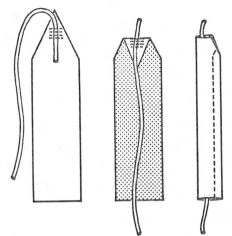

Stitch the strips (folded lengthwise, right sides together) to a width of ⅜ inch (a good ⅛-inch seam). Press the seam open (press the whole thing flat with the seam centered). Turn the strip right side out and press again.

If you ever make pants of corduroy or some other heavily piled fabric, make the belt loops considerably wider to facilitate turning. And turn from the end that will result in pulling with the nap rather than against it.

You have a choice between "regular" and "drop" loops. Both begin at the waist edge; regular loops disappear into the waistband seam, and drop loops are sewn to the pants ¼ inch lower. Regular loops take belts up to 1½ inches wide; drop loops, up to 1¾ inches. If the pants are to be worn with a wider belt, cut the loops longer by whatever amount the belt exceeds 1¾ inches, and attach the loops (drop style) that much lower.

For drop loops, do nothing now. For *regular* loops, cut the strips into seven lengths of 2¾ inches. Pin six of the loops in place, right sides together and with the top end even with the waist edge of the pants: 2 to 2½ inches from the fly seam, at the front of the outseam, and ¾ inch to the back of the dart.

Join the WAISTBAND (raw edge) to the pants in a good ¼-inch seam (suiting to suiting only.) Trim any excess from the ends of the waistband even with the pants. Turn the waistband (and the regular loops) up to finished position, and press open the seam.

If the ZIPPER needs to be shortened, measure it against the right pants front: When fully closed the slide fastener should be just below the waistband seam. At ⅛ inch above the level of the fly notch, hand sew the zipper teeth together over and over, using either button-and-carpet thread or waxed buttonhole twist. About an inch below the stitches, cut away the zipper end. Use old scissors. The blades will find their way between the zipper teeth. Open the inch or so of zipper below the stitches, and remove the teeth with needlenose pliers. (Pliers are also useful for pulling a needle through obstinate cloth—I keep a pair with my sewing tools.)

Baste the zipper right side down against the outside of the right pants front, putting the edge of the zipper tape back just a bit (1⁄16 inch or less) from the pants edge. At the top, angle the end of the zipper tape out over the seam allowance so it will disappear into the seam.

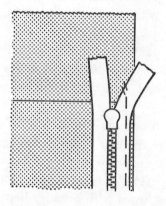

Get out the RIGHT FLY, the upper fly facing, and the fly lining. Join the upper fly facing to the lining in a ¼-inch seam, having the facing even with the convex side (outward curve) of the lining. Press the seam allowances down.

Match the convex side of the fly to that of the fly facing/lining, right sides together, with the seam in the facing/lining ¼ inch below the level of the fly notch. Stitch along the convex side in a scant ¼-inch seam. Press the seam open (over the handle of your shears), but do not turn it right side out yet.

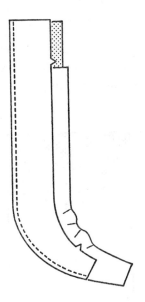

Baste the concave side of the fly, right side down, over the zipper, with the fly back just a bit from the edge of the zipper tape. (All this "back just a bit" is to bevel the seam allowances so you don't get a hard ridge from having all of them exactly on top of each other.) Working from the other side, stitch ⅛ inch from the zipper teeth (a good ¼-inch seam), starting at the fly notch and going all the way up, including the waistband. Remove bastings and press the seam open.

On the back side of each waistband, chalk a straight line ⅜ inch from the outer edge of the selvage (or at the inner limit of the selvage if its width exceeds ⅜ inch). On the right waistband, continue the chalk line across the top of the fly (but not its facing).

Caution: Have you preshrunk the CANVAS STRIP? It really shrinks!

Lap a canvas strip (the firmer edge if one is ripply) over the waistband selvage to the chalk line, and stitch a good ⅛ inch from the edge of the canvas, or midway of the ⅜-inch lap. At the front end of the left waistband, the canvas strip should be ¼ inch shorter than the band (so it will go to the seam but not into it).

If you are making a WATCH POCKET, get out the pocketing piece and the two watch pocket facings. With the pocketing right side down and the facings right side up, stitch a facing selvage ¼ inch onto each end of the pocketing.

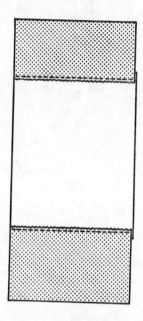

Fold up the pocket with the facing selvages on the outside. Seam the sides at a good ⅛ inch, starting ⅜ inch below the top. Clip in to the first stitch from each side.

Turn the pocket right side out, and stitch the side seams at ¼ inch.

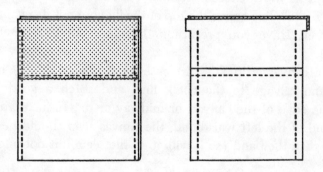

Trim away the ⅛-inch side protrusions so you have a plain rectangle.

The watch pocket goes against the inside of the right pants front, ¾ inch from the outseam. With the pants upside down, fold the top ⅜ inch of one of the pocket facings down out of the way, and stitch the inside of the other (uppermost) facing to the pants side of the waistband seam allowance in a scant ¼-inch seam.

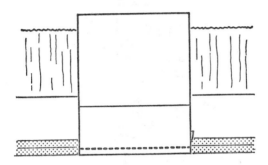

Turn the pocket down to normal position, and press it flat. The other facing will be sewn to the waistband side of the seam allowance as part of a later seam.

If you have *regular* belt loops, allow some slack and machine tack their upper ends in line with the seam between the waistband and the canvas.

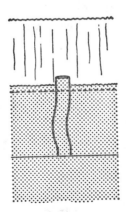

Regular style

For *drop* style belt loops, cut the strips into seven 3-inch lengths. Pin six of them to the pants, right side up and with the top end of each loop even with the selvage edge of the waistband (or, if the selvage is overly wide, down by whatever amount it exceeds ⅜ inch): 2 to 2½ inches from the fly seam, at the front of the outseam, and ¾ inch to the back of the dart. Stitch in line with the seam between the waistband and the canvas.

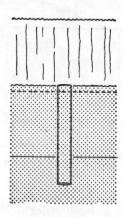

Drop style

Turn under the raw edge of each front pocket and fell it by hand to the outseam seam allowance. The coat board is a good foundation to work on. For an exceptionally neat result, instead of felling in the usual way (entering the needle in the outseam and bringing it up through the folded edge of the pocketing), do it this way:

Thread two strands of silk thread (waxed) into a needle as if you were going to sew with a single strand (so the needle will slip along the thread as you work and not wear through it in a single point of strain). Hide the knot by taking the first stitch from inside the pocketing fold straight out at the crease. At that very spot, enter the needle in the suiting seam allowance and let it emerge straight forward in the seam allowance, *at* the pocketing crease but not in it. In other words, take the stitch only in the seam allowance.

Take the next stitch only in the pocketing, entering straight into the crease opposite the last stitch, running forward within the crease, and exiting straight out from it. Continue to alternate the stitches in this way between seam allowance and pocketing. The

Ladder stitch

stitches can be any length so long as each is begun exactly opposite the end of the preceding one, and the seam will appear to have been sewn from the inside. This stitch is sometimes called a "ladder stitch." It is good not just for felling but for repairing rips that can't be got at underneath, for example in a lined coat.

Smooth flat the dangling tops of the front and hip pockets, and tailor baste them against the waistband seam. Just three or four stitches will hold each pocket.

Measure each WAISTBAND LINING against the waistband and mark (with pins or chalk) the positions of the back dart, the outseam, and midway of the front. Fold each CURTAIN in half lengthwise, right side out, and press in the crease. If you have not pinked these pieces, it is a good idea to overcast together the long side edges of the curtain. Join this double edge of the curtain in a good ¼-inch seam to what will be the lower edge of the waistband lining, pinching in three tiny (⅛ to ¼ inch) pleats in the curtain at the positions marked on the lining. Press the seam open and the pleats flat.

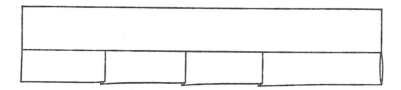

Waistband lining joined to curtain

Match the top edge of the waistband lining to the selvage of the waistband, right sides together, placing the pleats where they belong, and baste using a running stitch.

On the *right* half of the pants, fold back (up) the end of the waistband lining even with the seam containing the zipper. If you have folded back more than ½ inch, trim to about that amount. Fold back the fly facing over the fly, right sides together, and baste.

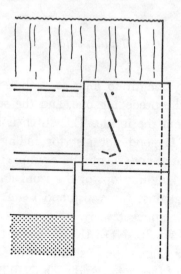

Working from the other side, you are going to stitch along the waistband at the edge of the canvas but not on it: On the *right* half, begin as part of the seam between the fly and its facing, round the corner (chalk around a nickel or a quarter or a small spool as a guide), and stop about 2 inches shy of where the crotch seam will be (center back). Around the corner, trim the suiting seam allowance to a scant ¼ inch (ripping back the straight seam as necessary), and trim the corner of the canvas round so it will fit into the seam when turned right side out.

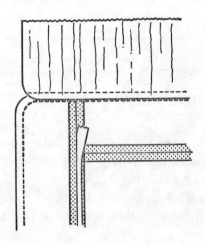

On the *left* half of the pants, start the seam 2 inches shy of center back and stop about 1 inch before the front end of the band.

Remove the basting and press open the seam between the waistband and the lining. Turn the lining to the inside and baste about ½ inch from the waist edge, easing the seam slightly to the underside. On the right leg continue basting along the seam between the fly and its lining.

With the lining and curtain turned up out of the way, smooth the waistband over the canvas, and from the outside run a basting just below the waistband seam, through all thicknesses except the lining and curtain.

With the lining and curtain still up out of the way (also the fly facing when you get to it), from the outside stitch within the waistband seam for its full length: If you have a watch pocket, deviate to just above (about ⅟₁₆ inch) the waistband seam as you stitch across the pocket, and securely tack (stitch back and forth) each end of what will be the watch pocket opening, ¼ inch inside the pocket outline. Rip open the waistband seam to make the pocket opening.

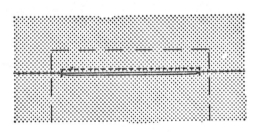

Watch pocket opening

Remove the lower basting and the tailor's basting at the tops of the pockets. Clip the canvas nearly up to the seam: midway of the fronts, at the outseams, at the back darts, and about midway of the darts and center back.

On the left pants front at the fly notch, cut inward in the seam allowance (of the front, not the fly) to the first stitch of the fly seam. Turn the fly to the underside and baste close to the fold. For the time being, leave the upper end of the fly dangling, but turn the seam allowance at the end of the waistband over the canvas and baste it flat.

It is time for the HOOK AND EYE: Thread about a 4-inch length of linen tape through the large opening in the hook and stretch the tape ends back together.

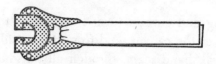

Center the hook inside the left waistband about ¹⁄₁₆ inch from the front. With button-and-carpet thread or waxed buttonhole twist (one strand) sew the hook and tape to the canvas, taking care the stitches don't go through to the outside.

Turn under the seam allowance the rest of the way up the dangling fly (front and top), slip it under the hook, and fell it to complete the fly seam and about ¾ inch across the top: no more. You aren't through under there yet.

If you are preworking the buttonholes by machine, work one now in the top of the right fly before installing the eye in the right waistband (through waistband and canvas) about ⅛ inch from the fly seam.

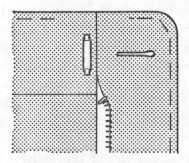

Some eyes have a hole in each end for sewing them in place. For this type you need to make holes through the waistband and canvas using an awl or an ice pick, poke the eye through from the outside, and sew its ends to the canvas on the underside. Other eyes have sharp prongs to be poked through and bent flat on the underside over a protective metal plate. It is a good idea to reinforce this latter kind by sewing each end to the canvas after it is installed.

Turn under the raw edge of the fly lining and baste so it barely covers the seam allowance and zipper tape. If necessary to make it lie flat, clip the seam allowance of the lining in several places along the curve. The lining tail remains loose at this stage, but you can baste the rest of the way around it, turning under about ¼ inch.

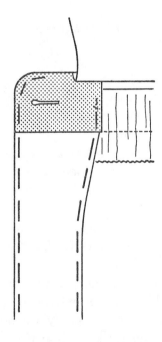

The fly lining secured

From the outside, stitch on the right pants front about ¹⁄₁₆ inch from the fly seam for the length of the zipper, including the lining underneath.

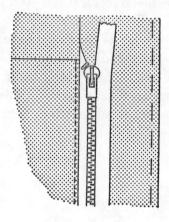

Right front topstitching

This is where the pants cease to be plural: Close the zipper and hook the hook. Lap the front edge of the left pants front to ¼ inch beyond the seam containing the zipper (a chalk line may help) and baste, making sure the inseams line up at the crotch. Working from the underside, baste the zipper tape flat against the left fly, angling the upper end of the tape back from the front of the pants. Remove the basting that holds the left front lapped over the right, open the hook, and stitch the zipper tape to the fly: Stitch first at the outer edge of the tape and again about ⅛ inch from the zipper teeth.

On the outside of the left pants front, chalk a guideline for the FLY TOPSTITCHING: 1½ inches from the front edge at the top, following the general outline of the fly around the lower part, and straight over to the seam for ½ inch at the fly notch. You will be stitching the left front to the left fly along the guideline. Tailor baste the two together in preparation.

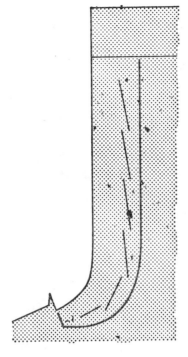

Fly topstitching guideline

With the zipper open and the right pants front pushed out of the way, start at the top and stitch all but the last ½ inch. Keep in mind that the pants are fragile at that spot, and resist the temptation to try them on until they are secure. A TRY-ON is misleading anyway until everything has been sewn in place and pressed flat.

Stitch the INSEAMS: Remember you allowed ½ inch along the back, so place the front edge that far from the back, and stitch from the front side in a good ¼-inch seam. Press the seams open, and turn the legs right side out.

If very much time has elapsed since you started the pants, re-check the man's waist measurement before you stitch the CROTCH SEAM. Pin the waistbands together at center back (¼ inch inside the thread marks), hook the hook, and verify the waist measure of the pants. Open the hook and the zipper, and stitch the crotch seam to a little past the inseams, stretching it firmly as you stitch. (It will stretch in wear, and you don't want the stitches to pop.) Stitch a second time for strength.

The last inch or so of the crotch seam is easier to stitch from the other side. Just below the zipper, because of the lap, you will be taking a ½-inch seam on the right pants front and a ¼-inch seam on the left. Stitch right up to the zipper end. Remove the crotch reinforcement bastings, and press the crotch seam open.

Attach the CENTER BACK BELT LOOP: Place the loop right side up over the seam in the waistband, with the top of the loop a good ⅜ inch from the top of the waistband. Stitch several times about ¹⁄₁₆ inch from the top of the loop. (To keep the loop from sliding off position while you stitch, start in the middle and take the first few stitches backward.) Turn the loop up, and stitch again to cover the raw end.

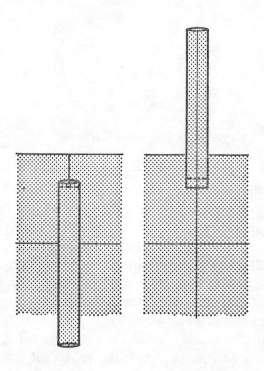

Align the lower end of the loop barely above the waistband seam for regular style, or ¼ inch beneath it for drop style, and stitch on that end. Pull the loop down over the raw lower end and stitch again, in line with the waistband seam for regular, or ¼ inch lower for drop style. Press in finished position.

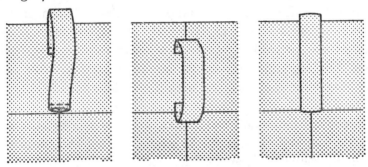

Center back belt loop

If your loops are drop style, affix the lower ends of the other six as you did at center back.

Fell the lining tail to the crotch seam allowance and/or the crotch reinforcement.

Stitch the last ½ inch of the fly topstitching, at the lower end of the zipper, back and forth several times.

Restitch the ends of the front pocket openings (to include the backs of the pockets).

At center back, with a double strand of silk thread, fell the crotch seam allowance along the waist edge and at the ends of the waistband.

Turn under and fell the ends of the waistband linings and curtains: at the back, even with the center back seam; at the right front, even with the fly seam; and at the left front, back enough to clear the zipper teeth but to cover the top end of the zipper tape (about an inch from the front end of the waistband).

Smooth the waistband lining down taut over the waistband, and run a basting above the curtain seam. Lift the curtain and sew its seam allowance (where you can get to it) to the canvas in a running stitch, backstitching every other stitch. The tailors call this a "back-and-fore" stitch. It consists of taking two running stitches at a time, always beginning behind the last stitch.

Smooth the curtains down, and with a few hand stitches sew each pleat to one thickness of pocket.

A practice BUTTONHOLE or two may be in order before you hand work the ones in the pants. Practice in a double thickness of outer cloth with a layer of muslin or pocketing between. If you are preworking by machine, do that and cut the buttonhole open. If you are not preworking, baste the layers together close around where the buttonhole is to go, make the cut, and prepare to carry along two strands of buttonhole twist as a filler under the working stitches.

Thread a needle with one strand of buttonhole twist, and wax only the last ½ inch or so of the strand. Do not knot it. Enter the needle on the left side at the back end of the buttonhole (not the eyelet end). When you pull the strand through, the waxed end will tend to stick in the cloth. Take the first few stitches over the thread end, and then cut it close.

For the second stitch, enter the needle close beside the first. Take hold of the thread behind the needle, and pass the thread around the point of the needle in a clockwise direction.

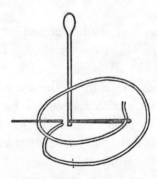

Pull the needle through. In drawing the stitch tight, pull the thread flat against the cloth, straight out to the side, so the knot (purl) is placed on the cut.

Continue in this fashion until you near the eyelet end. As you start around the curve, pull each stitch increasingly less flat, until at the end you are pulling straight up. Reverse the process for the far side of the eyelet. What this does is allow you to take closer stitches around the eyelet without crowding the knots. When you get all the way around to the back end, sew two strands (through and through) the width of the buttonhole and overcast them in a miniature bartack.

You can improve the shape of a finished buttonhole by manipulating the eyelet with an awl or something like the handle of a crochet hook. And to preserve the shape, baste the buttonhole closed whenever the garment is sent to a dry cleaner.

Hand-worked BARTACKS are an extremely nice touch at the ends of the front pocket openings in pants. They always receive attention out of proportion to the little trouble they take, and they are a sturdy reinforcement for these points of strain. Bartacks are made just like the back end of a buttonhole: With a single strand of buttonhole twist, make two through-and-through stitches over the machine tacking, and overcast with shallow stitches.

Remove any residual basting and PRESS the pants thoroughly, paying particular attention to the inside of the waistband and the crotch seam. Press in the BACK CREASES no higher than the crotch: Lay the legs together and press the upper limits as one, to insure that they stop at the same height. When the pants go to a dry cleaner, caution him not to lengthen these creases—there is nothing pretty about a sat-on crease.

Sew on the BUTTONS, using either button-and-carpet thread or waxed buttonhole twist. Take the stitches over a pin so the button will stand away from the cloth for neat fastening. If you like, you can wind the thread around a few times under the button before tying off, but a "shank" is not really necessary with the flatness of fine tailoring.

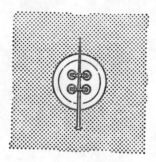

If the pants are made of some cloth that won't ease well (corduroy, denim, a woven man-made fiber), don't try to angle the leg BOTTOMS. But, if the cloth is wool, you can make the bottoms ½ inch shorter in the front: Flatten the legs at the creases and cut straight, removing ½ inch at the front crease and nothing at the back. Overcast the bottom edges.

If you are not making cuffs, just turn up 2 inches (1¾ if you angled the bottoms) and baste. The pants length is the one thing you can verify in a fitting before you put in the permanent stitches.

If you are making CUFFS, refer to the inseam and outseam notches that indicate the finished length of the pants. At a cuff's depth lower, chalk a line around the outside of each pants leg parallel to the bottom. Chalk a second line a cuff's depth below the first.

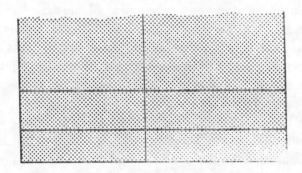

Along the upper chalk line, fold up the pants bottom to the inside of the leg, and baste about ½ inch from the fold. From the inside, run a second basting on the other chalk line through both thicknesses, keeping the seams aligned even if you angled the bottoms.

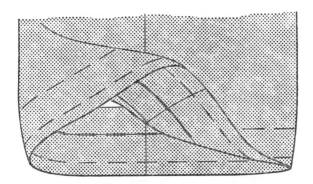

Turn up the cuff on the second basting, letting the raw edge go to the inside. Baste near the bottom fold, through all thicknesses.

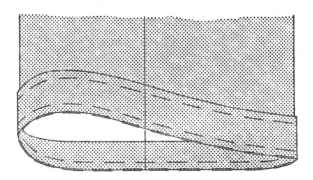

Even in hemming the bottoms, a tailor does something a little bit special. Have you ever noticed that hems are inclined to show through in thicker cloth like wool suiting and doubleknits? The stitches pull and dimple the cloth. The reason is that, in both of the commonest methods of hemming (the old-fashioned hemming

stitch and the cross stitch), the thread passes from the outside of
the turn-up, over its edge, exerting a pull against the right side.

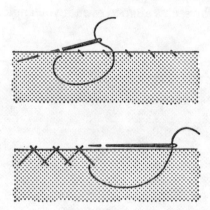

The solution is to place the thread *between* the layers of
cloth: Run a basting about ¼ inch below the edge of the turn-up.
Bend the overcast edge down at the basting while you work, and
proceed in the old-fashioned way, barely pricking the outer layer.

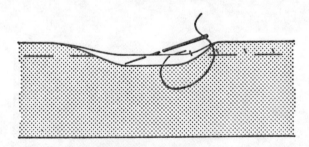

Hemming the bottoms

In the try-on be severely critical with the aim of refining the pattern. So often in sewing for a woman you solve the intricacies
of a pattern only to put it away and go on to the different problems of another style. Sewing for a man depends on three or four
basic patterns, well worth perfecting because of their continued
usefulness.

Consider again each of the pants measurements. Is the amount of ease in the seat optimum? Is the man satisfied with the vertical proportioning—the overall length, the height of the waistband, the room through the crotch and seat? If he complains only of a slightly close feel through the crotch, urge him to wear the pants a few days and see whether they become more comfortable as they stretch with wear.

Write on the pattern any proposed improvements or comments, and date your note.

Having satisfied yourself as to the fit, encourage him to comment on the style. Most men are not accustomed to being able to dictate the details of their clothes, and it may take him a while to realize he can now afford to think about such things. And now that you have actually produced something wearable, he may be more interested in the particulars.

Ask him about the length of the pockets—does his billfold fit in at the height he likes? (In these pants you can shorten the pockets by stitching across the bottom.) Would a different spacing of the belt loops be better?

The chances are it will be some *little* thing that determines whether he is totally pleased. It may be something about the fit, or it may be the bartacks, or the roominess of the pockets. For one of my students it was a buttoning detail of the hip pockets copied from an old pair of pants. For another it was a special pocket for a pocketknife added to the inside of the right front pocket— her beautiful tailoring went almost unnoticed while her husband admired that little patch of cloth inside his pocket.

It is amazing how much you can change the overall effect by varying some detail of style. And there really is a lot of choice in design. Take advantage of every opportunity to examine good clothes. Visit the best menswear shops, and make a note of what you see. A sketch book of style details becomes a source of inspiration.

Maybe this is your first experience in juggling patterns. Part of the fun of sewing is that it can be a medium of expression and not merely a mechanical reproduction of a pattern. Not only can you make a pattern, if that's what it takes to get a good fit, but you can take an existing pattern (commercial or your own) and vary it in unlimited ways. Each new approach in styling lends itself to a number of subtle VARIATIONS. Here are a couple of idea-starters for you:

Front pocket openings are sometimes offset from the outseam in a slant.

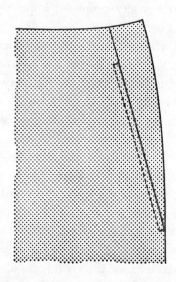

While an extreme slant may be associated with casual pants, a slight one can result in a more formal effect because it has less tendency to bulge than does a vertical opening.

These are the pieces that are cut differently: the pants front, front pocket, pocket facing, and pocket extension. Rather than mutilate the pattern, cut out the front and the pocket by the pattern, and then change the cloth pieces: On the front, chalk a straight line beginning at the lower pocket notch and angling in at the waist whatever distance pleases you. Indicate a notch 6½ inches up in the slant.

Trim the front along the chalk line, retaining both notches, and trim the front half of the pocket (the side with the corner cut away at the top) to match. Cut away the new pocket corner, ¾ by ¾ inch.

Use the scrap you trimmed from the front as a guide in cutting the facing, which must be in line with the grainline of the front instead of on a selvage. The facing is ⅜ inch longer than the scrap at the bottom, and 2 inches wider up to ½ inch above the upper notch; from there to the top, it is ½ inch wider than the scrap.

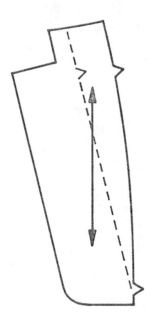

The extension is rectangular, cut on a selvage, 7½ by 2 inches. On the facing, overcast the outseam side and the long straight edge. Or, on the straight edge, if the cloth is lightweight and you prefer, press under ¼ inch.

The construction is very similar to what you are already familiar with.

Lay out the front pocket right side up. Over it lay the pants front, also right side up. Place the raw edge of the extension right side down over the angled edge of the front, and baste a length of linen tape ¼ inch from that edge. Stitch on the outer edge of the tape, notch to notch.

At the notches cut inward to the last stitch. Remove the basting and press the seam open. Turn the extension to the underside, baste, and topstitch notch to notch at ¼ inch.

Stitch the selvage of the extension to the pocket. Place the facing across from it, even with the top of the pocket and ⅜ inch from the side. Join the facing to the pocket along the long straight side and part way around the bottom.

Close the pocket with a french seam, as in front pockets that follow the outseam.

Above the pocket opening, turn the pants front back over the facing and from the pants side, with the pocket pushed out of the way, stitch the seam (¼ inch) that completes the slant. On the facing, clip in diagonally to the last stitch and press the seam open.

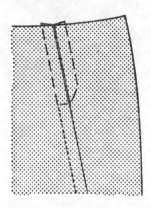

On the front side of the pocket, just above the french seam, cut inward ½ inch, as before. Stitch crosswise at each end of the topstitching, omitting the back side of the pocketing at the bottom but including it at the top.

The outseam follows the overcast edge of the pocket facing, and the back side of the pocket is felled to the outseam seam allowance, as in pockets with outseam openings.

A different approach in hip pockets is a lower edge piping that is an inverted flap.

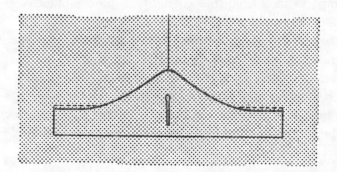

The following pieces are cut the same as for a regular hip pocket:

pocket, of pocketing (7½ by 16½ inches)
upper edge facing, of silesia (1 by 7 inches)
one rectangular facing, of outer cloth (7⅛ by 2⅛ inches)

The flap, cut with the grainline of the pants back, is 7⅛ inches wide by 1 inch high at the ends. At the center, it rises ¾ inch. Its facing (outer cloth) is cut the same as the flap but 2 inches deeper and on a selvage.

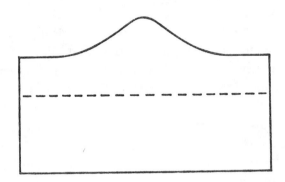

Chalk the position of the pocket on the pants back. Lay the pocketing, right side up and selvage end down, underneath the back with the pocketing ¾ inch higher than the chalk line. Baste the two together on the line. Place the upper edge facing right side down above the line, and stitch at ¼ inch, observing the 6-inch limit.

Baste a length of linen tape to the back side of the pocket flap a scant ¼ inch from the long straight line. Join the flap to the flap facing in a ¼-inch seam along the curved side only—end to end. Press the seam open, but do not turn it right side out.

Lay the edge of the flap that has the linen tape face down, beneath and touching the chalk line on the back. Stitch on the outer edge of the tape, the same distance as the upper seam.

Tie the thread ends. Remove the bastings and press open the lower seam. Trim the seam allowance slightly around the curve, and turn the flap right side out. Baste close to the curved edge.

Press, remove bastings, and press again. From the outside, stitch within the lower seam, including the flap facing underneath.

Cut the pocket open, and complete it by the regular hip pocket instructions.

As your pants making becomes more frequent, you may find it helpful to have cardboard patterns for the auxiliary pieces, such as the pocket tab, upper fly facing, hip pocket facings, and the watch pocket and its facings. A tailor usually has a collection of these patterns hanging on a nail near his cutting table.

Another aid is a cardboard HIP POCKET GUIDE to make it easier to mark the right and left pockets identically. Cut the guide 6 inches wide and 3 inches high, with a slight curve in the top to conform with the waist, and with a notch in the center of the straight bottom edge to be matched to the point of the dart.

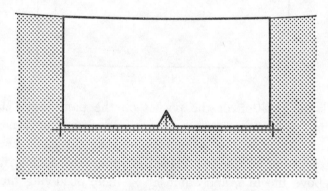

Hip pocket guide

The best suggestion I know for speeding up pants making came from a man who made all the coats and suits for himself, his wife, and their several children. That in itself might not be remarkable, but this man worked five days a week as a guard in a government building. Nights he worked unloading produce for a food market. Saturday mornings he worked as a barber, and Saturday afternoons he tailored. His advice for streamlining pants making is: Don't ever make *one* pair of pants.

It is dramatically faster to make several simultaneously than to make the same number serially. In the cutting out, you chalk only the first pair and cut subsequent pairs by the cloth pieces of the first. And, in the making up, it is only the first time through an operation that you have to think or consult instructions; repetitions are automatic.

CHAPTER 7

Very Casual Pants in a Hurry

Now that you know what is involved in making fully tailored pants, let's explore some ways to cut corners.

The tailored HIP POCKETS are the most obvious place to compromise. You no longer need to be told they are intricate and time consuming. Even though they come so near the beginning, their completion very nearly marks the halfway point in cutting out and making pants. I have heard a tailor call them "the only tailoring in pants." The substitution of patch pockets in the back, then, takes a sizable chunk off the working time.

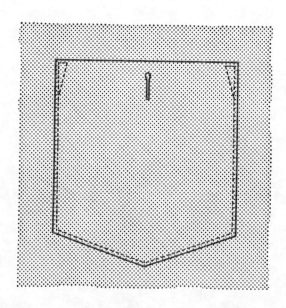

Patch pocket stitching should be reinforced at each end of the pocket mouth by including a patch of linen tape on the back side.

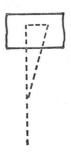

The traditional FRONT POCKETS (with opening either in line with the outseam, or offset from it at an angle) are probably the easiest way to lend distinction to pants that are otherwise stripped of unnecessary details. If the outer cloth happens to be suitable, a shortcut within the traditional method is to cut the front pockets from the outer cloth and make them right side *in*. That way there is no need for pocket facings or extensions and no felling at the outseams. For the first seam, the pockets are joined to the outside of the pants fronts, right sides together, with linen tape over all. Then they are turned to the underside and closed in the usual way. The back layer of the pockets and the first little bit of the french seams are included when the outseams are stitched.

If you make patch pockets in the front, you may want to consider a shape easier to get into than one with a horizontal opening. One possibility is the style made popular by jump suits. (See illustration page 112.)

For a pocket in this style, cut a lining the same shape as the pocket and stitch the two right sides together along all edges except the top and the short vertical side. Turn the pocket right side out and topstitch the curved mouth. Attach the pocket to the pants front along the long vertical side and the bottom. The top and short side are included in the waistband seam and outseam respectively.

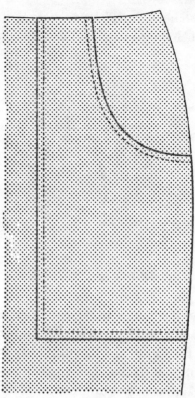

BELT LOOPS are expendable. A beltless waistband that fits is a comfort seldom experienced by a man who is dependent on ready-made clothes. The reason is that commercial beltless pants usually adjust to a range of waist sizes instead of fitting any one. It is fortunate that pants in this style are so easy to make, because custom-tailored ones tend to be addictive.

With a continuous WAISTBAND the fly is cut only as high as the upper notch, and the upper fly facing is eliminated. The curtain too can be dispensed with, as can the separate waistband lining. There is no need to break the waistband at center back, because allowance for alteration can come from the projection at each end of the band in the front. So, instead of two waistbands, two waistband linings, and two curtains, you cut one piece, on a sel-

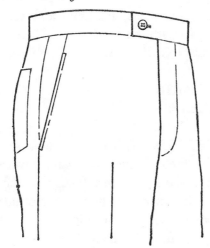

vage of the outer cloth: in length, the waist measurement plus 5¾ inches. (for a projection of 1½ inches at each end); and in width, twice the waistband width, plus ½ inch.

This waistband treatment is suitable for any outer cloth, and it can be quite handsome made up in something like a worsted flannel. But it is especially desirable in WASHABLE pants, because the canvas is enclosed.

In washable pants, another consideration is the thread: Cotton or cotton/polyester is preferable to silk, because silk dyes are not color fast.

After the various deletions, the pieces are:

> 2 fronts
> 2 backs
> 2 flies
> 1 waistband
> 1 fly lining
> 1 fly interfacing
> 2 crotch reinforcements
> 1 waistband interfacing (canvas strip)
> the pocket pieces

OVERCAST the outseams, inseams, and rise, adding in the crotch reinforcements with the fronts.

Press in the FRONT CREASES.

Make the PLEATS, if any.

Stitch the back DARTS.

Make the POCKETS.

Stitch the OUTSEAMS.

Attach the LEFT FLY (with the interfacing), stitching all the way up. Make the second "tucking" seam. Overcast together the raw side and end of the fly and interfacing. At the fly notch, in the pants front seam allowance, clip in to the first stitch. Turn the fly to the underside, and baste near the edge.

Baste the ZIPPER face down against the outside of the right pants front, allowing room at the top for a waistband seam of a good ¼ inch.

Join the RIGHT FLY to the fly lining along their convex sides in a scant ¼-inch seam (the tops are even). Baste the concave side of the fly right side down over the zipper. Stitch from the other side, taking a good ¼-inch seam.

Turn the right fly and its lining right side out, and baste near the edge. Turn under the raw concave edge of the fly lining and baste just covering the zipper tape and seam allowance. From the outside, stitch on the pants front, about 1/16 inch from the seam containing the zipper.

Lap the front edge of the left pants front to ¼ inch beyond the seam containing the zipper, and baste. From the underside, baste the zipper tape to the left fly. Stitch at the edge of the tape and again about ⅛ inch from the zipper teeth.

Do the FLY TOPSTITCHING, omitting the last ½ inch at the fly notch, as before.

Stitch the INSEAMS and the CROTCH SEAM.

Fell the lining tail, and complete the fly topstitching.

Cut the CANVAS waistband interfacing to a length of the waist measurement plus 4¾ inches, and trim the width to the finished waistband size. Lay the canvas against the inside of the WAIST-BAND a scant ¼ inch from the selvage and ½ inch from each end. Stitch the length of the canvas, ¼ inch from each side. Continue stitching parallel lines ¼ inch apart for the full width of the canvas.

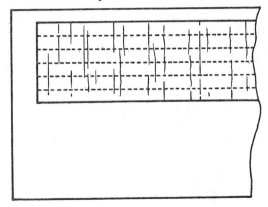

Join the long raw side of the waistband to the waist edge of the pants (right sides together) in a good ¼-inch seam, allowing the band to extend 2 inches at each end. (Because of the fly, the center back seam of the pants does not match the center of the band, so you will have to fold the pants to find the halfway point.) Press the waistband and the seam allowance up.

Fold the interfaced portion of the waistband to the inside, and run a basting midway of the band. Turn in and fell the seam allowance of the waistband projections, but, for the rest of the way of the band, leave the selvage edge out.

From the outside, stitch within the waistband seam, to include the selvage of the waistband underneath.

Remove bastings and PRESS, including the BACK CREASE.

Finish the BOTTOMS.

At each end of the waistband, work a BUTTONHOLE, the one on the right to attach to a button on the inside of the band. Sew on the BUTTONS.

To adapt the pattern for SHORT PANTS, determine the desired inseam length and the pants leg circumference at that length. On the pattern, mark off the inseam, measure the discarded length, and mark off the outseam correspondingly.

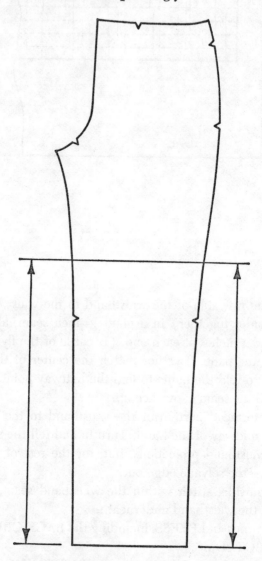

For short pants

The width of the front bottom should be half the circumference, and that of the back should be half plus 1 inch. Make any change equally at the outseam and inseam to preserve the balance of the pattern. (Illustration next page.)

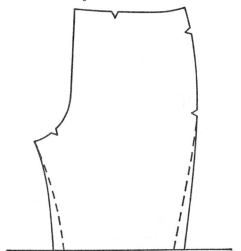

Changing the bottom circumference

One place I'd like to suggest you not cut corners is the bottoms of short pants. If a short bottom is to be horizontal in the wearing, it must be cut in a curve that meets the outseam and inseam in a right angle. Allow a seam's width at the bottom, and cut a separate facing, to be attached with the familiar "tucking" seam. Hem as for long pants.

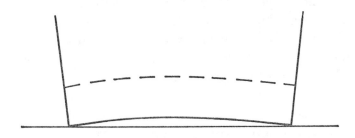

Shaping the bottom of short pants

With simple styling and construction, it is still possible to keep the quality high. Often the details that make the difference are little or no additional work; for example, crotch reinforcements, fly interfacing, and linen tape in the pocket openings and to reinforce patch pocket stitching. When you cut corners, take care to retain these little extras.

CHAPTER 8

Cutting Out the Coat

Unlike the situation with pants, in coat making it is not necessary to begin with a drafting square and pencil to have an adequate pattern. For a coat, the advantages of using a commercial pattern outweigh the drawbacks. Besides the obvious saving in time, there is the advantage that commercial patterns reflect current styles. Pattern catalogues are revised monthly, while a tailor's style book may not be updated for several years.

Whereas the ⅝-inch seam allowance of a commercial pattern is unwieldy in pants, it is welcome in a coat. The variety of seam widths on a tailor's coat pattern is confusing to a beginner. A consistent ⅝ inch is a good compromise.

The whole concept of fitting has been revolutionized within the past ten to fifteen years. At one time each pattern company had its own set of measurements, with size varying from brand to brand. Eventually a common standard was adopted, and a few years ago pattern sizing was made to conform with ready-to-wear. This progress took only sixty to seventy years, and even the pattern companies don't seem to appreciate what they have finally done.

Now that sizing has been standardized, elaborate measurement charts and personalized basic patterns are obsolete. They are also misleading. Pattern dimensions depend on more than body size. Allowance for ease varies with style and general cloth weight—a summer-weight suit pattern, for example, is drafted closer than a winter one. To think in terms of pattern measurements, therefore, has its pitfalls. To know that a certain style and weight jacket measures so many inches around the seat is of interest only in that particular jacket. But to know that a size 38 jacket is 1 inch too tight through the seat is of far-reaching consequence.

When you buy a pattern, you pay somebody else to take into account a long list of measurements and circumstances. Your job is limited to knowing what size to buy and what changes to make— not what the pattern measures or what it ought to measure, but the difference between the two. The establishment of routine pattern changes is the key to simplicity in fitting.

No matter how they are arrived at, first changes must be considered estimates. The important thing is that they be precise, known amounts, with wide seam allowances of a known amount for correction and refinement. Even the experts achieve perfection in a pattern through a process of evolution. A tailor makes changes in a suit pattern at least through the third or fourth suit.

While it is true that the sizing of ready-made clothes is undependable, the fit of the better ones is at least an indication of how to change a commercial pattern to make it fit. Try on coats in "regular" sizes (not "talls" or "shorts") until you determine the size that

Alteration of coat length

fits best through the neck and chest. PATTERN ALTERATIONS will then be simple ones in length or width.

Fitting is something you will eventually do almost by feel. The underlying system depends on specific estimates and on distributing those estimates in such a way as to preserve the balance of a pattern.

Study the lengthwise proportioning of the ready-made coat. Judge not just the overall body length but whether the waist suppression (indentation) is at the proper level. Estimate any proposed change in pattern length and whether it should be made above or below the waist level, by folding out extra length or by cutting and spreading the pattern pieces to add length. (See illustration preceding page.)

Similarly, judge whether to alter the sleeve length above or below the elbow, or both.

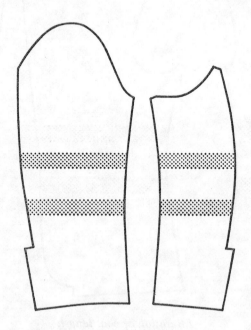

Note the shoulder width, which is altered by reshaping the upper armhole of the front and the back.

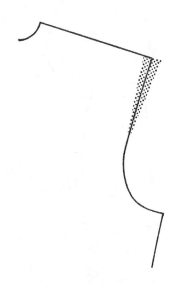

The set of the collar is of interest only as an indication of what to expect in the fitting. Any change in collar height is made after the fitting, and the pattern is altered only after the first coat is completed. There are two reasons for this postponement. One is the danger of overaltering, which would result in distortion. And the other is the difference in fit of a ready-made coat and a hand-shaped one—a difference nowhere more apparent than in the collar.

Compare the hip measurement on the coat pattern envelope with the seat measurement for your pants pattern, and alter the bottom of the coat pattern accordingly. Because the pattern covers half the body, the total pattern change is half the difference in the two measurements. Make half the change in the back (at center back and the side seam) and half in the front (at the side seam only) to avoid distorting the side seam.

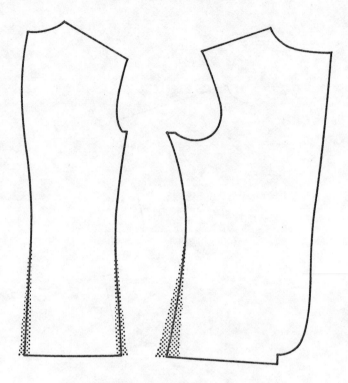

Alteration of coat width at the bottom

If you ever draft a coat pattern with the aid of a tailor's style book, these are the MEASUREMENTS you will need:

Chest   _____   _____
Waist   _____
Seat   _____
Armhole (scye) depth   _____
Waist length   _____
Coat length   _____
Back width   _____
Shoulder slope   _____
Strap   _____
Blade   _____
Sleeve inseam   _____

Coat measurements are taken over a shirt. The first step is to determine where to take the chest measurement, which is in line with the armhole depth. Put one of your hands rather heavily on the man's shoulder to make sure he doesn't hold his arm abnormally high, and with your other hand hold a ruler horizontally under his arm as high as a coat sleeve would be comfortable. Place a pin on his shirt to indicate that height.

Fasten a piece of tape or ribbon around the man's chest with the top edge of the tape in line with the pin. Make sure the tape is level, and leave it in place for the duration of the measuring.

The CHEST measurement is taken over the tape or ribbon, about the same tightness as the seat measurement for pants. Record the reading, and beside it write half the amount, which is "scale" for a coat pattern.

The WAIST and SEAT measurements are the same as for pants.

The zero point for lengthwise measurements is the nape, the most prominent spot on the spine at the back of the neck. Pin a second length of tape or ribbon so it hangs down center back with a mark at the nape.

The ARMHOLE DEPTH is the distance from the nape to the top of the chest tape. On the coat pattern, it is measured from the collar seam at center back to the level of the bottom of the armhole seam.

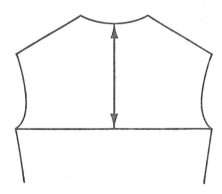

Armhole depth

WAIST LENGTH is measured from the nape to the waist level; and COAT LENGTH is the total length from nape to coat bottom.

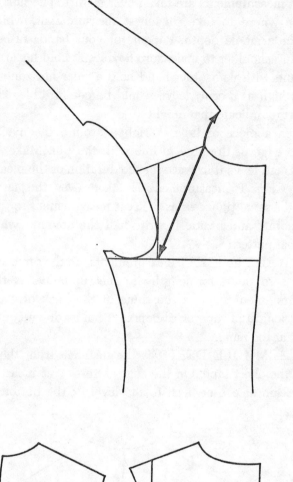

Strap

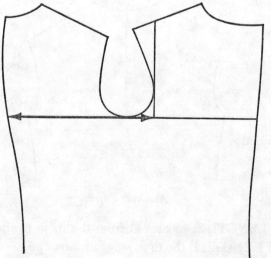

Blade

The outer limit of the shoulder seam is at the acromion. Slide your finger up over the rounded top of the arm until you feel a little hollow just above the upper end of the arm bone. That hollow is the acromion. Measure straight across the back between the outer limits of the shoulder seams (BACK WIDTH), and note the distance from the nape (SHOULDER SLOPE).

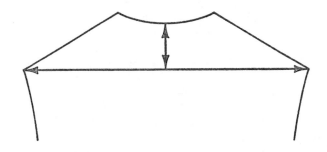

Back width and shoulder slope

Some drafts also ask for a back width taken midway of the armholes.

Hold a ruler vertically at the front of the armhole, and mark the point where it touches the top of the chest tape. The STRAP is measured from the nape around the collar seam and straight across the shoulder to that point on the tape.

The BLADE is the distance from center back at chest height to the same point to which you measured the strap.

And the SLEEVE INSEAM is most easily taken from a coat.

The coat pieces that are cut from the OUTER CLOTH are:

> 2 backs
> 2 fronts
> 2 side fronts (if separate)
> 2 front facings
> 2 upper sleeves
> 2 undersleeves
> 1 upper collar, blocked out as follows:

Lay the UPPER COLLAR pattern on a fold of the outer cloth (neck edge up if the cloth has an up and a down). Cut a rectangle well outside the pattern outline, and cut away the corners of the neck edge. The upper collar gets no further trimming until after it has been shaped to the coat.

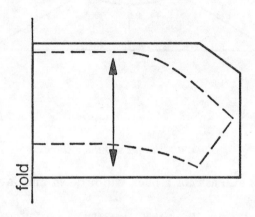

Upper collar

The pocket facings and flaps (if any) are cut later from scraps.

If the PATTERN PLACEMENT is crowded, you can ease the situation by trimming the lengthwise sleeve seams to ¼ inch, with the vents ¾ inch wider. If the side front is separate from the front, their joining seam can also be reduced to ¼ inch. But the side seams and center back should be left intact to allow for alterations. If you make any of these changes, write yourself a note and pin it to the cloth pieces.

On each front, THREAD MARK the bridle line (roll line), center front, and the positions of the pockets and the buttons and buttonholes. Use a ruler to chalk the lines, and run a contrasting thread in each front. (Illustration next page.)

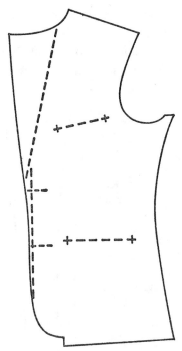

Thread markings

Unless the cloth is loosely woven, there is no need to OVER-CAST edges because the coat will be fully lined.

STAYSTITCHING offers no security (because thread too can stretch) and is best omitted as a reminder that bias edges are vulnerable until safely seamed.

If the outer cloth lacks body, it is a good idea to UNDERLINE the upper back: Cut two pieces of muslin by the back pattern, extending to several inches below the armhole, and baste one to the underside of each half of the back. Throughout the construction, the muslin is treated as one with the outer cloth.

The LINING is cut (with pinking shears if you have them) by the pieces of outer cloth as follows:

The SLEEVE linings are an inch shorter and have no vents; otherwise they are identical to the coat sleeves.

The BACK lining is cut full length, with vents if any, and with a 1-inch seam allowance at center back. Allow an extra ½ inch at the shoulders.

The FRONT lining equals the coat front minus the front facing, plus 1¼ inches (two ⅝-inch seam allowances).

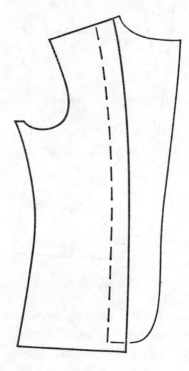

Front lining

If there is a separate SIDE FRONT, cut the lining separately also. (Some commercial patterns combine front and side front in the lining.) Indicate any front darts (also sometimes omitted). These "extra" seams are helpful in attaching the lining to the coat.

With the outer cloth and lining cut out, you are ready to sew. Interfacings and pocket pieces will be described in their place in the construction.

CHAPTER 9

Putting the Coat Together

Stitch any DARTS in the fronts, and join fronts to SIDE FRONTS if those pieces are cut separately, in preparation for making the LOWER POCKETS. Directions are given for three pocket styles: double-piped (which look like big bound buttonholes), flap, and patch.

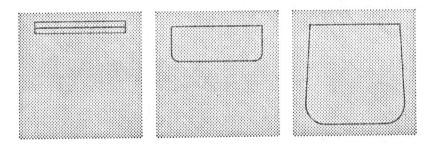

Front pocket styles

If you are making either double-piped or flap pockets, cut an 8-inch depth the full width of the silesia, and slit the fold to make two pieces. From the raw end of one piece, cut 4¼ inches. Lay aside the two larger pieces, which will become an inside (lining) pocket and a breast pocket later. The little piece 8 by 4¼ inches will be a change pocket inside the right lower pocket.

For DOUBLE-PIPED pockets, cut another 8-inch depth the full width of the silesia and slit the fold. Also cut two lengthwise strips of silesia, 8 by 1½ inches. And on a selvage of the outer cloth, cut six 8-inch facings, two each in three different widths: 1½, 2, and 2½ inches.

Stitch the selvage of a 2-inch facing, right side up, a good ¼ inch onto the raw end of each of the two lower pocket silesias. At the selvage end of *one* silesia, stitch a 2½-inch facing in like manner. This will be the left coat pocket.

Half an inch from the selvage end of the other (right pocket) silesia, chalk a 3¾-inch line, centered. Cut along the line, and at the ends cut inward ⅜ inch, at a right angle to the line. Match an end of the CHANGE POCKET silesia, right sides together and centered, to the cut. From the back side, stitch the two together ³⁄₁₆ inch from the cut.

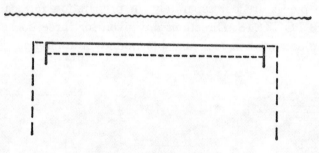

Press the seam open. Push the change pocket silesia through the opening to the back side, folding at the limits of the end cuts so you leave a ⅜-inch gap in the large silesia. From the back side, stitch within the seam.

Fold up the dangling end of the change pocket so it overlaps the raw (upper) side of the opening by a good ¼ inch. Stitch midway of the lap. From the right side, stitch the pocket outline through all three thicknesses, rounding the corners at the bottom. Slit the change pocket fold, and trim the seam allowance at the rounded corners. (See upper illustration next page.)

Lap the selvage of the other 2½-inch facing onto the end of the pocket silesia, covering the ⅜-inch gap and even with the mouth of the change pocket. Stitch on the facing selvage. If your machine zigzags, stitch a bartack at each end of the change pocket opening. (Lower illustration next page.)

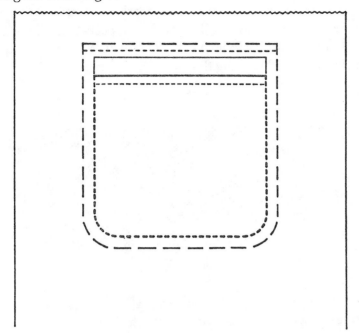

Change pocket construction

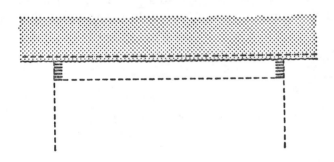

Change pocket opening completed

The right and left pocket silesias are attached alike. The procedure is similar to the way a regular hip pocket is made in pants. In fact, if you are making a coat without having made pants, turn back to the directions for a hip pocket and make a practice one from scraps. Practice pockets are routine for a tailoring apprentice. They are the standard way to prevent difficulty and mistakes in a garment.

On the outside of each coat front, mark the center 6 inches of the thread-marked guideline for the lower pocket opening. Lay a strip of silesia (8 by 1½ inches) underneath the coat front, and baste the two together along the line.

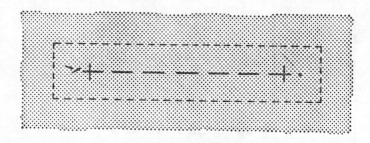

Lay a 1½-inch facing right side down above the line with its long raw side touching the line. Baste a length of linen tape a scant ¼ inch above the edge. Stitch on the lower edge of the tape, within the limits of the 6-inch line.

Lay a 2-inch facing (attached to a pocket silesia) face down beneath the line with its 8-inch raw side touching the line. Baste a length of linen tape a scant ¼ inch from the edge, and stitch on the upper edge of the tape, the same distance as before.

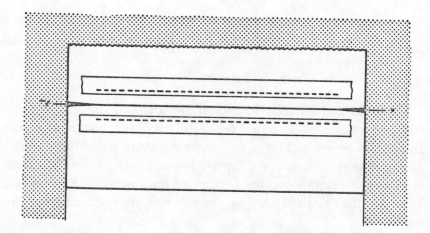

Examine the back side to be sure the lines of stitching are parallel and ½ inch apart.

Press both seams open. Turn each facing snugly over its seam allowance to form a piping, and baste, making the basting no longer than the seam. From the right side, stitch within the lower seam only, to include the facing underneath.

Holding the facings out of the way, cut through the coat front and the reinforcing strip of silesia, midway between the two seams and curving to the last stitches. Push the pocket and both facings through to the underside, and stitch the ends of the pocket opening, as in a hip pocket.

On the back side, fold up the dangling end of the pocket about ⅛ inch lower than the selvage of the upper facing (to bevel the layers for flatness) and baste. From the outside, stitch within the upper seam.

Stitch the pocket outline, beginning at the ends of the pocket opening and widening a bit at the bottom. Make the bottom 1½ inches above what will be the finished lower edge of the coat. Trim the seam allowance of the back of the pocket to a good ¼ inch and that of the front a little wider.

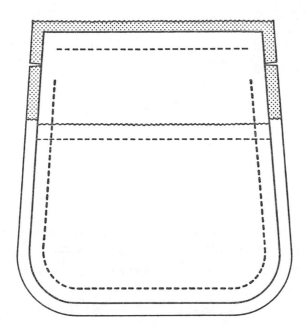

For FLAP pockets, first decide on the size and shape of the flap. Add ⅜ inch to the length and the width to allow for seams (a good ⅛ inch all around). Cut two flaps from the outer cloth (matching the grainline of the coat front) and two from the lining. From the silesia cut two pocket pieces: in length, half the width of the silesia, and in width, the finished width of the flap plus 2 inches. Also from the silesia, cut two lengthwise strips the width of the silesia pocket pieces by 1½ inches.

On a selvage of the outer cloth, cut two facings the width of the pocket silesias by 2½ inches. And from the lining, cut two similar facings: crosswise if the lining has a cloth design, lengthwise if not.

Stitch the selvage of a facing of outer cloth, right side up, a good ¼ inch onto the raw end of each pocket silesia.

Two inches from the selvage end of *one* of the pocket silesias, lay a facing of lining right side down. Stitch ¼ inch from the edge of the facing so that, when turned up, the facing covers the end 2¼ inches of the silesia. Press in that position. This will be the left pocket.

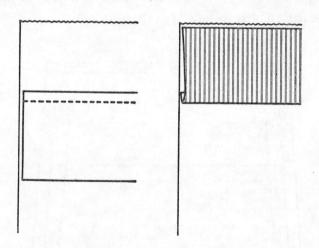

At 1⅞ inches from the selvage end of the other (right) pocket silesia, chalk a 3¾-inch line, centered and parallel to the selvage. Cut along the line, and at the ends cut inward ⅜ inch at a right angle to the line.

Make the CHANGE POCKET as described above under double-piped pockets. Attach the remaining lining facing to the change pocket end of the silesia with the facing seam at the mouth of the change pocket.

Make the pocket flaps: Join each to its lining in a good ⅛-inch seam, leaving open the top, by which the flap will be attached to the coat. Press the seam open, and turn the flap right side out. Ease the seam slightly to the underside, and baste about ¼ inch from the edge. Press, remove bastings, and press again.

Lay a 1½-inch-wide strip of silesia (cut earlier) underneath each coat front, centered with the thread-marked guideline for the lower pocket. Baste along the line. (See upper illustration page 132.)

Position a flap, lining side up and open edge down, above the line so the open edge is a scant ⅛ inch over the line. Be sure the flap width is centered against the guideline. In other words, you can make the width of a flap whatever you choose so long as you respect the midpoint indicated by the pattern designer. Join flap to coat front in a ¼-inch seam.

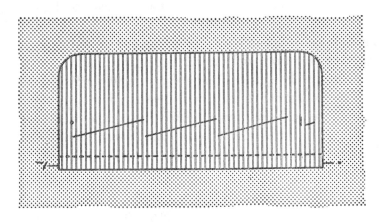

Attaching the pocket flap

Both pocket silesias are attached in the same way, which is similar to the procedure with a regular hip pocket in pants.

Lay an outer cloth facing (with silesia attached) right side down with its raw edge at the flap *stitching*. Baste a length of linen tape a good ¼ inch from the facing edge. Stitch on the upper edge of the tape, making the limits correspond with those of the flap stitching. Remove bastings.

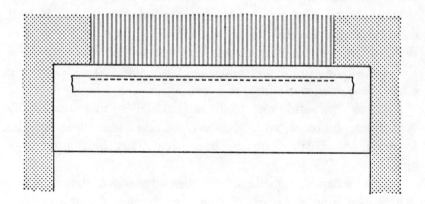

Examine the back side to verify that the two lines of stitching are parallel and ⅜ inch apart.

Press open the lower seam. Fold the facing snugly over its seam allowance, and baste beneath the seam. From the outside, stitch within the seam including the facing underneath and forming a piping.

Cut the pocket open: Hold the facings out of the way and cut through the coat front and the reinforcing strip of silesia, midway between the two lines of stitching and curving to the last stitches.

Push the pocket silesia and the flap seam allowance through the opening to the back side, and stitch the ends of the pocket opening, as in a hip pocket. Press the flap down and its seam allowance up.

From the back side, cross stitch the flap seam allowance to the silesia strip.

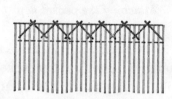

Securing the flap seam allowance

Fold up the dangling end of the pocket to about ½ inch above the pocket opening, and baste. Slip the flap inside the pocket. From the outside, stitch within the flap seam to include the back side of the pocket underneath.

Stitch the pocket outline, as described above under double-piped pockets (page 133).

The following is a really superior PATCH pocket method that I have often used to upgrade a shirt or unlined jacket.

Choose a pleasing pocket shape and cut a pattern, allowing a generous turndown at the top (at least 1½ inches for a lower coat pocket) and ¼ inch around the sides and bottom. For the coat, cut out two pockets from the outer cloth, matching the grainline and cloth design, if any, of the coat front. On each pocket, mark the fold line, either by chalking both sides or by running a contrasting thread.

Fold the pocket pattern on the fold line, and cut out the lining by the portion of the pattern that is a single thickness, plus ½ inch at the top.

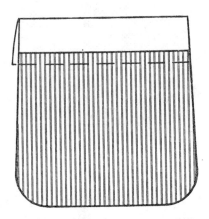

On each pocket (outer cloth) fell a length of linen tape to the underside of the turndown at the fold line.

Join lining to pocket in a ¼-inch seam along the straight top side only. Press both seam allowances toward the lining.

In the outer cloth only, starting at the fold line, stitch ¼ inch from the edge around the sides and bottom. Clip in ¼ inch at each side midway of the turndown.

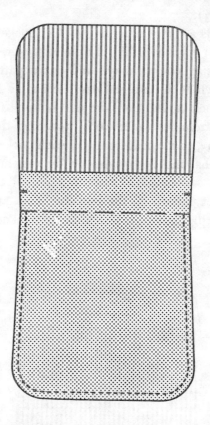

Turn under the ¼-inch seam allowance around the pocket (outer cloth), from midway of the turndown. Baste, encouraging the stitching out of sight. Press, clipping around the curve if necessary to get a smooth outline.

Fold the pocket at the fold line, right sides out, and baste close to the fold. Tailor baste the pocket to the lining, keeping the stitches well back (at least 1¼ inches) from the edge. (See illustration next page.)

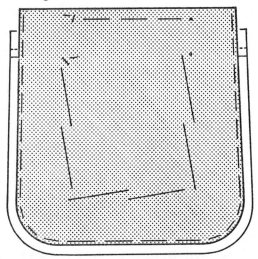

Trim the lining layer of the pocket to 1/16 inch smaller than the outer layer. Lay the pocket on the coat front, with the top of the pocket centered against the thread-marked guideline. Lift the outer layer of the pocket, and join the lining layer to the coat by stitching 1/8 inch from the raw edge. Begin at the fold line, and tack the stitches well there (stitch back and forth), including a patch of linen tape underneath the coat front.

Fell the sides and bottom of the outer layer to the coat front, covering the lining. Make the stitches invisible by taking them slightly under the edge of the pocket and by using a ladder stitch.

In a traditional BREAST POCKET, the opening is about 1/2 inch lower at the front end. The pocket welt is cut from outer cloth, 5 inches wide and 1 1/8 inches deep, with a 5/8-inch turnback at the top. The welt matches the grainline of the coat front.

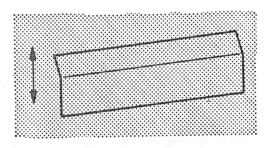

Breast pocket welt

Cut a second strip 1¾ inches deep, at the same slant as the welt.

On the welt, run a contrasting thread to mark the fold line. Fell a length of linen tape to the back side of the ⅝-inch section at the fold line.

Get out the smaller of the two silesias that you cut and laid aside when you cut the lower pockets. Lap the selvage end, right side up, a good ¼ inch onto the right side of the ⅝-inch section of the welt, and stitch on the selvage, including the linen tape underneath.

Fold the welt at the fold line, right sides together, leaving a little crosswise slack in the welt as it lies against the silesia. With the tape side down, stitch the ends of the welt at ¼ inch, stopping ¼ inch before the bottom of the welt and tacking the stitches there.

At the ends of the welt, trim the seam allowance of the tape side to a scant ¼ inch, and in the silesia only, cut diagonally down to the last stitch.

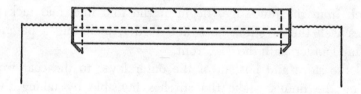

At each end of the fold, trim the corner. Turn the welt right side out, and baste near the fold and ends. Press, remove bastings, and press again.

Place the pocket assembly upside down, with the right side of the welt against the coat front. Fold the silesia down to expose the raw edge of the welt. Join welt to coat in a ¼-inch seam, stitching along the thread-marked guideline in the coat front.

Press the seam open, and tuck the welt seam allowance inside the welt to be hidden by the silesia. From the outside, stitch within the seam, including the silesia underneath.

With the coat front unfolded and right side up, pull the pocket silesia down at the seam. Lay the 1¾-inch strip right side down with its lower edge against the welt seam. Stitch a good ¼ inch from the lower edge of the strip, starting and stopping ¼ inch inside the limits of the first seam.

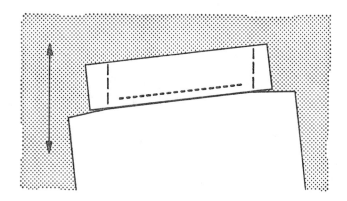

Cut the coat front midway between the two lines of stitching, stopping even with the shorter (upper) line and cutting up and over to the last stitches.

Pass the silesia and the strip through to the back side of the coat front. Press the upper seam open.

Fold up the dangling end of the silesia to about ⅝ inch higher than the raw bottom of the strip, and slit the silesia fold. This unattached piece of silesia is the back of the pocket. Turn the top edge under at ¼ inch, lap it a good ¼ inch onto the right side of the strip, and stitch.

Stitch the pocket outline, making the depth 5¾ inches, the sides vertical, and the corners at the bottom rounded. Trim the seam allowance.

Fell the welt sides and ¼ inch of the top of each end of the pocket opening (ladder stitch). Pass the needle through to the underside, and backstitch diagonally between the first and last of the stitches, taking care you don't go through to the outside.

Stitch and press open the CENTER BACK and SIDE SEAMS. If you have a vent in any of these seams, stop the stitching at the top of the vent, and reinforce the end of the stitching with a patch of linen tape on the underlap side.

And now you come to the foundation—literally—the CANVAS FRONT. This is tailoring in the grand old manner with quality the aim.

The trend to iron-on interfacing represents progress in the same way a cake mix improves on a butter-and-eggs cake: The work is reduced a little, and the quality a lot. Yet this trend to commercialization has invaded some of the larger tailoring establishments, making them little better than factories. When iron-on interfacings are employed commercially, however, there is this distinction from the home variety: The "tailors" are investing in expensive equipment to make the process work; they are not using a hand iron. One way of looking at the situation is that you can no longer afford the equipment to make a cheap coat, while all you need for a fine one is a needle and thread and a little know-how.

The superiority of hand-sewn shaping lies in its flexibility and its insistence. The sewn shape is an exaggeration, which in pressing is reduced to the desired degree. Thus the coat, instead of losing its shape between pressings, is always seeking to accentuate it.

The components of the canvas front are cut from hymo, haircloth, felt, wadding, and muslin.

The HYMO is a slight abbreviation of the coat front pattern, with the same ⅝-inch seam allowance. Cut it just to the front of any seam between the front and the side front. Chalk the bridle line on both sides of both pieces, and mark any darts.

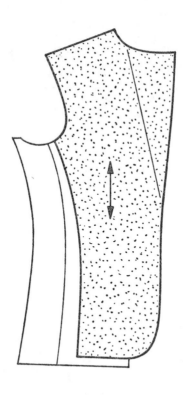

Hymo

The HAIRCLOTH is cut about ½ inch smaller than the hymo at the neck, shoulder, armhole, and side, and about ⅛ inch smaller at the bridle line. The grainline is the same as that of the hymo (and the coat front), *not* parallel to the bridle line, as it would be if you were interfacing without shaping.

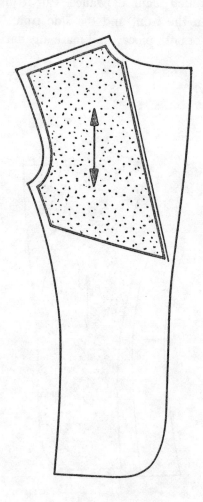

Haircloth

The FELT is cut by the shoulder and armhole of the hymo, about 4 inches wide at the front, long enough to overlap the haircloth about ½ inch at the bottom, and about 3 inches wide at the back.

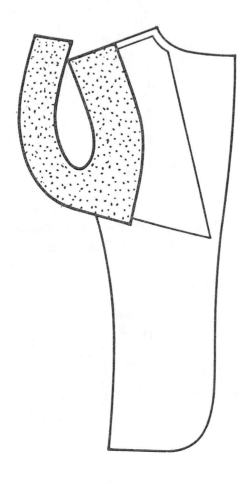

Felt

From the sheet of WADDING, cut a strip 5½ inches wide. Cut the strip into six 5½-inch squares, and divide the squares diagonally to make twelve triangles. Also cut two felt triangles the same size as those of wadding.

In the hymo, cut along the seam lines of any darts. Draw the cut edges together, center a 1-inch bias strip of muslin underneath, and sew back and forth across the cut.

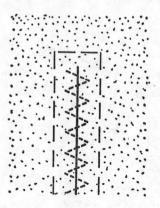

Closing a dart in the hymo

Midway of the shoulder, slash the hymo to a depth of about 4 inches, and spread the cut ⅜ inch. Place a scrap of hymo underneath, and sew about ⅛ inch from the sides of the cut. Trim the scrap to a wedge shape.

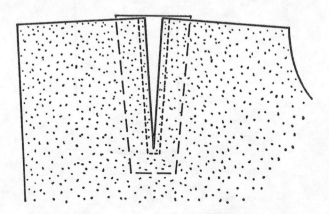

Shoulder gusset in hymo or haircloth

Cut into each haircloth shoulder about 3½ inches. Spread the cut a good ¼ inch, and patch it with a scrap of haircloth.

Lay out each piece of hymo, smooth side down (strips and patches up), and build up the canvas front in this order:

Lay the haircloth, smooth side down, over the hymo. Center a

1-inch bias strip of muslin over the bottom and front edges of the haircloth, and baste (big stitches). The purpose of the muslin is to protect the coat from being rubbed by the sharp edges of the haircloth. Place a felt triangle at the shoulder, long side even with the hymo armhole, and square corner at the haircloth shoulder.

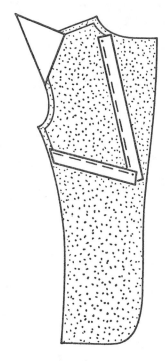

Building up the canvas front

Arrange six triangles of wadding with the short sides staggered but the long ones coinciding, so the thickness trails off to nothing everywhere but the long side.

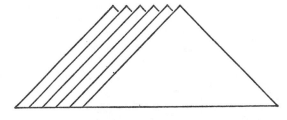

Arranging the wadding triangles

Center them over the felt triangle, even with its long edge.

Place the felt piece over all, shoulder and armhole matched to the hymo, and baste using a few scattered, loose stitches. You want the layers free to shift during the shaping.

The basis of the shaping process is this: When two (or more) layers are bent, there is slippage between their surfaces because the outer layer has farther to go.

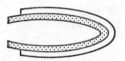

To shape the canvas front, you bend it and sew the layers together at the bend. Then you rebend a little to the side, and sew on that bend. Finally all the bends add up to a curve.

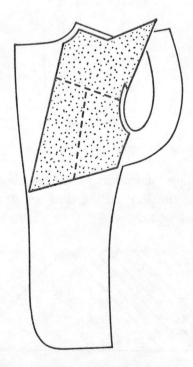

Canvas front—area to be shaped

The smooth side, which is outermost during the shaping, is the one that will eventually be placed against the inside of the coat front. The shaping is applied to the area of the canvas front that has more than one layer. That area is treated in three sections, as illustrated on the bottom of page 148.

The shoulder section is the first to be shaped. Midway of the arm-hole, fold the canvas front horizontally, smooth side out, and run a length of through-and-through tailor's basting at the fold. Use one strand of basting thread, and make the stitches firm but with no more pucker than can be pressed out. Refold at a slightly higher level, and sew back in the other direction. Continue in this manner, working always on the edge of the fold, until you have completed the shoulder section.

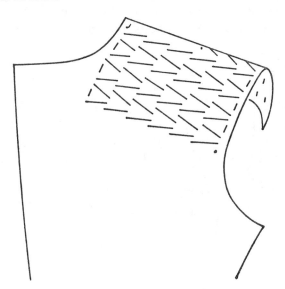

Shaping the shoulder section

The remaining two sections are sewn vertically. Fold the canvas front lengthwise in the middle, and sew on the fold. From the middle, work your way to one side. Then turn the canvas front upside down, go back to the middle, and shape the final section.

When both fronts have been shaped, dampen them with a sponge and press with the help of the coat board. In the pressing, accentuate the shape by shrinking at the armhole and along the bridle line.

Hang the fronts upside down (you can pin them to the edge of the pants board or ironing board), and allow them to dry completely. In fact, once they have been pressed, refrain from laying them down.

Press the body of the coat itself, stretching crosswise at the shoulder, and shrinking at the armhole and bridle line, as you did with the canvas front.

Situate each canvas front underneath the appropriate coat front, and baste coat to canvas along the bridle line. Baste exactly on the line, because the basting will later identify the bridle line from the inside. Continue basting the length of the front about an inch from the edge.

Lay the coat front over the coat board, and run a second line of (tailor's) basting a little back from the first. Continue across the front, smoothing coat to canvas and basting every few inches. As you come to darts and the ends of pocket openings, turn the coat

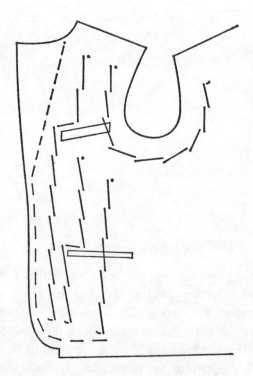

Basting the canvas front to the coat

to the inside and take advantage of their seam allowances to attach the canvas permanently. Use the same basting thread, but take care that the stitches don't go through to the outside. Finally, situate the felt around the back of the armhole, and baste about 2 inches from the shoulder and the armhole.

On the inside of the coat, stretch a length of linen tape at the back side of the bridle line, following the earlier basting.

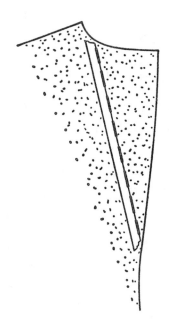

Baste the tape to the canvas (and coat), using widely separated backstitches and pulling the tape tight enough to ripple the canvas and coat slightly. With a single strand of waxed silk thread, fell the outer edge of the tape, taking the stitches through the canvas and slightly into the outer cloth of the coat underneath. At the neck and front, the canvas will eventually be trimmed to about ⅛ inch back from the coat seam line, so keep the hand stitches within that limit. Fell the inner edge of the tape to canvas only.

The next step is to pad-stitch the REVERS. It may be that you have been referring to this area as a "lapel." The lapel is the part of the coat that is *lapped* in the wearing, while the revers is the area to the outside of the bridle line, the part that is *reversed,* or turned over, from inside to outside.

The revers is shaped, or pad-stitched, in the same way as the canvas front with these differences: The thread is silk (one strand, waxed), and the stitches go through the canvas but only slightly into the outer cloth. The desired shape is a pronounced curl.

Fold the coat front at the bridle line, canvas side out, and sew the first row close to the bridle line and parallel to it. Take small

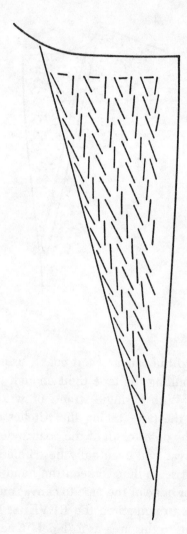

Shaping the revers

stitches, and keep one hand inside the fold so you can feel that the needle is not going through to the outside. Refold and work outward over the revers in fine, parallel rows, keeping back from the coat seam line a good ⅛ inch at the neck and front.

Over the canvas, baste linen tape at the inner side of the seam line: across the top of the revers, down the front of the revers and coat, and at least part way around the bottom. If the outer cloth has a loose weave, extend the tape all the way around the bottom of the coat at the hemline. Around the curve at the bottom of the coat, clip the inner edge of the tape to make it lie flat. And at the point of the revers, fold a miter in the tape.

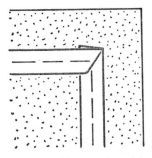

Mitering the linen tape

Trim the canvas just under the outer edge of the tape. Fell both sides of the tape with silk thread.

Press the coat, and hang it upside down.

Get out the LINING pieces and the front facing (outer cloth).

In the lining, stitch any darts and join the front to the side front, if those pieces are separate. Join the front facing to the lining front, stopping the seam about 2 inches from the bottom. Press the seam allowances toward the lining.

Trim the LINING POCKET silesia (cut at the same time as the lower pockets) to a width of 7 inches. Cut two lengthwise strips of lining, preferably on a selvage, 7 by 2½ inches.

With the silesia right side up, lay a lining strip face down across it with the raw side of the strip back 2 inches from the silesia selvage (as illustrated under flap pockets on page 134). Stitch strip to silesia ¼ inch from the raw edge of the strip, so that, when turned up, the strip covers the end 2¼ inches of the silesia. Press in that position.

On the outside of the lining for the *right* coat front, measure down 12½ inches on the facing seam. At that level, chalk a 5½-inch horizontal line, 1 inch on the facing and the remainder on the lining side of the seam, slanting down slightly at the front end. With the lining right side up, lay the pocket silesia right side down beneath it, so the lining-strip end is down and the raw end is ½ inch above the chalk line on the lining. Baste the two together on the line. (If the lining fabric is very delicate or easily marked by perforations, you may want to do the basting with a single strand of silk thread in a small needle.)

On the back side of the remaining lining strip, chalk a 5½-inch line 1 inch from the raw side. Place the lining strip right side down and selvage down over the front lining so the chalk lines on the two coincide. Baste over the first basting.

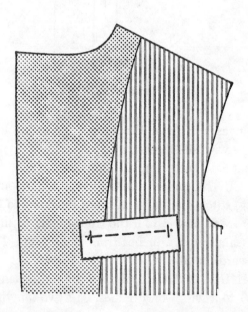

Stitch through all thicknesses a good ⅛ inch above the line, and again ⅜ inch below the first stitching. Cut midway between (on the chalk line), all the way across the lining strip, and curving to the last stitches in the coat lining and silesia.

Press both pieces of lining strip over their seam allowances, and turn them to the underside, forming pipings. Baste. Stitch the ends of the pocket opening, as in a regular hip pocket in pants.

From the outside, stitch within the lower seam, including the piece of lining strip underneath. Stitch the selvage of the lining strip to the pocket silesia.

Fold up the dangling end of the pocket silesia to about ½ inch above the pocket opening, and from the outside, stitch within the upper seam, including the pocket silesia underneath.

Complete the pocket outline, rounding corners and making the pocket 7 inches deep. Trim the seam allowance to a good ¼ inch on the back side and slightly wider on the front.

Join each half of the lining back to the front (or side front), but do not yet stitch the center back seam. Press the side seam open. On the back side of the front facing, turn up and press ¼ inch along the bottom 3 inches of the back side.

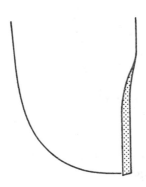

Join the front facing (with lining attached) to the coat front, stitching from the canvas side at the outer edge of the tape (not on it): At the top, begin at the outer limit of the collar (refer to the pattern), and tack the stitches. Stitch around the point of the revers in a tiny U instead of a V. Stitch the entire front edge of the coat, and around the bottom as far as the back of the front facing.

Clip in to the first stitch in the neck seam allowance of both the coat and the facing. Trim the seam allowance: Make it narrower on the coat side of the revers, and from there down, trim it narrower on the facing side. Press the seam open, and turn it right side out. Baste a good ¼ inch from the edge, easing the seam slightly to the underside: to the coat side of the revers and to the facing side from there down.

From now on, let the bastings collect in the coat until it is finished. These last in particular will be needed until the end, and many of the others will help the coat to resist the distortion it is subjected to in the making.

An attractive treatment of a VENT is to miter its turnback with the coat hem.

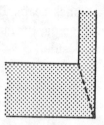

Turn up the hem, right sides together, and mark its height against the outside of the vent. From that height at the edge, chalk a line to the hemline, ½ inch (the turnback width) from the edge. From there, chalk a second line to the bottom, 1 inch (twice the turnback) from the side edge.

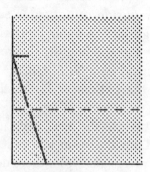

Fold the two lines together, and stitch. Turn the corner right side out.

Still on the underlap side, at the top of the vent, clip in diagonally to the last stitch in the vertical seam. Turn down the seam allowance of the top of the vent, and miter it with the ½-inch turnback of the side.

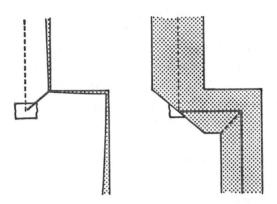

On the overlap side, turn back the full width of the vent, so the fold is a continuation of the vertical seam. At the bottom, miter the vent turnback with the coat hem.

Baste the hem and the vent turnbacks in a continuation of the front edge basting. Tailor baste about an inch back from the edge basting—around the revers, front, and bottom of the coat. Press the entire edge, using a damp cloth.

HEM the coat bottom and the sides of any vent, using the stitch recommended for pants bottoms (illustrated on page 102).

Situating a LINING is a methodical operation that involves a lot of basting. The progress is from the front toward center back.

From the facing side, with the revers turned back in finished position, smooth facing to coat and run a tailor's basting approximately at the bridle line. Lay the coat over the coat board, outside up, and baste about 3 inches back from the front edge.

From the facing side, run a basting just to the front of the seam between facing and lining. Turn back the lining, and sew the facing seam allowance to the canvas front, beginning 2 inches from the top. Use silk thread (double) and cross stitches, and avoid obstructing the lining pocket.

Continue basting and sewing as far as the side seam, keeping the stitches 2 inches away from the shoulder and armhole. Take advantage of all darts and pocket ends on the way to secure the lining.

Sew together the side seam allowances of lining and coat in a back-and-fore stitch (backstitching every other stitch). Roll up the coat out of the way on each side, and stitch the center back lining seam at ½ inch (not the full 1-inch seam allowance). Do not press the seam open. Turn the lining through to finished position.

Smooth and baste your way from side seam toward center back: Baste 2 inches from the armhole, shoulder, and neck. Remember, you allowed an extra ½ inch at the shoulder of the lining back. Baste across the back at about armhole depth and again at about waist level.

At center back, fold a one-sided pleat in the lining, and baste. If you have a center back vent, put the seam allowance of the lining pleat on the same side as the vent underlap.

Lining pleat at center back

On the overlap side of any vent, turn under the lining edge and baste it ⅛ inch from the side edge of the vent. Fell the upper portion, leaving the lining loose at the bottom.

Using two strands of silk thread, sew the top of the vent underlap in finished position, taking care the stitches don't go through to the outside. From the outside, sew the top of the vent in a backstitch, entering the needle only about a thread's width behind each previous stitch.

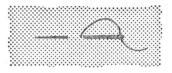

Backstitch

On the underlap side, turn under the lining edge at the top and side of the vent, and baste. Turn under the lining edge ½ inch above the bottom of the coat, and baste in a running stitch ½ inch above the lining fold.

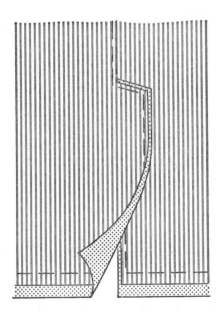

The next few bastings are in preparation for the fitting, after which they will be removed to return the coat to its present stage of completion. Caution: Do not attempt to try on the coat, or hang it up, until after the undercollar has been basted in place.

Baste the shoulder seams. Pull up the dangling end of the felt, and tack it to the canvas front. Smooth the front lining to the shoulder, and baste. Baste the shoulder of the back lining over the front.

Trim the UNDERCOLLAR cloth (melton) to the finished size and shape of the pattern. In other words, make no seam allowance except at center back, where you will join the two bias pieces. Cut the linen canvas the same size and by the same grainline.

In the melton, stitch the center back seam and press it open. In the canvas, lap the two halves and stitch, to avoid the thickness of a pressed-open seam. On the canvas, mark the roll line. Attach the canvas to the underside of the melton by stitching on the roll line.

The undercollar is pad-stitched in the same way as the revers, using one strand of waxed silk thread and keeping the stitches at least ⅛ inch back from the edge of the melton. The long, narrow portion below the roll line (the "collar stand") gets no shaping, but it is sewn in short, vertical rows of padding stitches so the two layers will adhere to each other.

In shaping, the undercollar is treated in three sections.

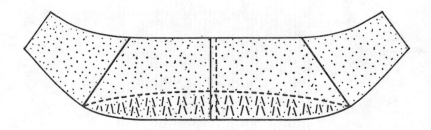

Work the center section first, beginning at the roll line and continuing in lengthwise, parallel rows that curl the undercollar in a long roll with the canvas on the outside. Work each end section crosswise, beginning at the end of the center section and working outward.

Press the undercollar over the coat board, and press a crease, canvas side out, at the roll line. Trim the canvas 1/16 inch back from the edge of the melton all around.

On the outside of the coat, chalk the neck seam line. Set the undercollar onto the coat: Lap the bottom of the collar stand to the chalked seam line, matching the end of the undercollar roll line to the bridle line on the coat, and baste.

TRY-ON the coat, being careful not to stretch the armholes. Pin the fronts together at center front. Besides the dimensions you considered before cutting out, there are two things to check in this fitting: the set of the collar and the hang of the coat.

Examine the upper back. The drape there can be drastically altered by a small change in collar height. A horizontal wrinkle beneath the collar may be erased by lowering the collar as little as ⅛ inch. If you think you need a ¼-inch change, try ⅛. In alterations a little goes a long way, and too much is worse than none at all.

If the hang of the coat is spoiled by a discrepancy in shoulder height, there are at least three methods of correcting the imbalance. A favorite of department store fitters (that is frowned on by the better tailors) is to add padding on the side of the low shoulder. A better approach is to curve the shoulder seams slightly, so that at mid-shoulder you take up more on the low side and less on the high one, while the shoulder seams remain the same at each end.

Only if the discrepancy in shoulder height is extreme should you think of lowering one armhole. In that case, slope the shoulder seam more steeply, and trim the bottom of the armhole to retain the correct armhole circumference.

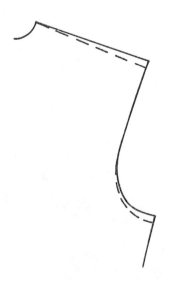

Correction for drastically *low shoulder*

If you make very much concession to a high or low shoulder, you may find the hang of the side seams affected. Taking in the high-side side seam near the bottom of the coat should correct that imbalance.

After the fitting, mark the neck seam line with contrasting thread. Remove the undercollar, and take out the bastings that were just for the fitting.

Stitch the SHOULDER SEAMS (outer cloth only) and press them open.

In the following, keep any stitches in the outer cloth at least 1½ inches back from the armhole. From the outside, with one hand held under the shoulder area of the coat, baste the coat front to the canvas front along the upper armhole, shoulder, and neck. The armhole edge of the canvas front will be trimmed later. On the inside, pull up the dangling end of the felt and tack it to the canvas front. Smooth the front lining up and sew it just behind the shoulder seam—permanently—to the canvas front (near the armhole) and the shoulder seam allowance (near the neck). Turn under the shoulder seam allowance of the back lining and baste it in place.

From the outside of the coat, where the neck seam line intersects the bridle line, stick a pin through to locate that point on the front facing. Through the point on the facing, chalk a straight continua-

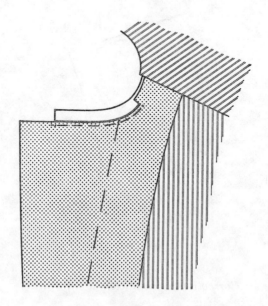

tion of the top of the revers, and continue chalking the seam line around the neck of the facing. On the facing, midway between the point (at the bridle line) and the shoulder seam, clip in to the chalk line; and from there to the front, tuck in the facing seam allowance and baste.

Set the undercollar onto the outside of the coat at the neck seam line, and baste. With silk thread, cross stitch the raw neck edge of the coat—including canvas front and lining—to the undercollar. Fell the neck edge of the facing where you tucked under the seam allowance and basted earlier. Re-press the crease in the undercollar, extending the crease to the first inch or so of the bridle line.

Dampen and press the blocked-out UPPER COLLAR, stretching about the outer two-thirds, fan-like.

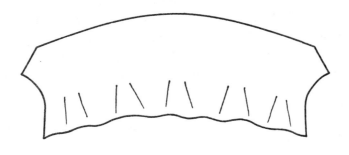

Upper collar shaped by pressing

Lay the upper collar right side out over the undercollar with the outer, fanned edge extending ½ inch. Baste on the collar roll line and ½ inch above the top of the revers. Baste a good ½ inch from the outer edge, smoothing the collar as you go. From the undercollar side, baste midway of the collar stand. Trim the upper collar seam allowance to ½ inch all around. Tuck it under and baste.

With two strands of silk thread, fell the neck edge of the upper collar, including where it joins the top of the revers. Change to a single strand and fell the edge of the melton all around in a simple overcasting stitch. Make the stitches close together, perpendicular to the edge, and as uniform as you can.

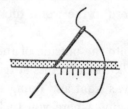

Felling the undercollar

Join each upper SLEEVE to the undersleeve along the under-arm seam.

From WIGAN cut two 4-inch-wide bias strips, each about 15 inches long, and press a slight curve into them. Lay a wigan strip across the underside of each sleeve so the wigan covers the hemline and extends about ½ inch into the hem allowance. Lift up one end of the wigan at the underarm seam and hand sew the wigan to one side of the seam allowance. Baste the wigan to the sleeve on the hemline. On each side, where the vent will be, run a thread to mark the seam line.

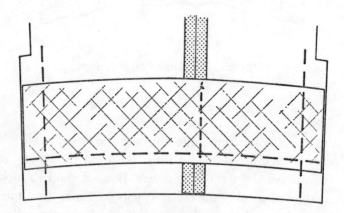

Wigan basted inside sleeve bottom

Stitch the other lengthwise sleeve seam, stopping 3 inches above the hemline.

On the undersleeve side of the vent, turn up the bottom at the hemline, right sides together, and stitch a ⅛-inch seam the depth of the hem.

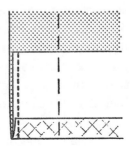

Sleeve vent, undersleeve side

On the upper sleeve side, miter the bottom as for a coat vent. *Do not trim* (in case the sleeve ever needs to be lengthened). Press open the seams at both sides of the vent and turn them right side out. Baste about ¼ inch from the fold at the hemline and the sides of the vent.

With silk thread, cross stitch the sleeve hem to the wigan. Press all around the sleeve bottom, using a damp cloth. Remove bastings and press again. Lap the vent to finished position. From the underside, backstitch diagonally from the end of the lengthwise seam to 1 inch above the hemline at the edge of the underlap, taking care the stitches don't go through to the outside.

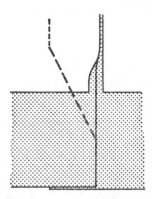

Finished sleeve vent, underside

At the seam line of the armhole edge, machine stitch with your longest stitch around the top of each sleeve, front notch to back notch. Leave the thread ends free for drawing up the sleeve cap fullness later.

Stitch both lengthwise seams in the SLEEVE LININGS and press them open. Lay out the sleeves wrong side out and undersleeve up. Lay over them the linings, wrong side out and undersleeve down, with the linings ½ inch higher than the sleeves at the top. Join linings to sleeves by hand-sewing their lengthwise seam allowances together, sewing no closer than 3 inches to each end of the sleeve seams.

Turn each sleeve with the lining side out. Turn under the lining hem allowance at 1 inch shorter than the sleeve, and baste ½ inch above the fold. Tailor baste the lining to the sleeve at about 3 inches from the armhole edge.

Set each sleeve into its armhole: With the sleeve right side out, turn the coat back over it and pin (outer cloth to outer cloth only) at the front, back, and shoulder notches. Push the sleeve lining down out of the way. Match sleeve to coat along the lower part of of the armhole, and pin at intervals.

Use the long machine stitching to draw up the sleeve fullness above the front and back notches. Match the sleeve to the coat along the upper armhole, and pin at intervals.

Stitch, with the sleeve side up so you can follow the long machine stitching. Concentrate on one section at a time, pushing the canvas front and coat lining out of the way underneath.

Trim the lower armhole seam allowance to a good ¼ inch, and press as stitched. Above the front and back notches, with the sleeve side up and the seam still as stitched, dampen and press out the sleeve fullness at the seam. At the front and back notches, clip the coat seam allowance. Press the seam open above the notches.

From the outside, with the sleeve lining pushed down out of the way, baste within the armhole seam through all thicknesses. With the sleeve seam allowance uppermost, backstitch around the armhole seam through all thicknesses—in the seam allowance but very close to the machine stitching—using two strands of basting thread.

Trim the armhole seam allowance (all thicknesses) to ½ inch at the shoulder, decreasing to a good ¼ inch at the front and back notches and around the lower armhole.

From the full width of the sheet of wadding, cut a 4-inch-wide strip. Fold the strip lengthwise so the edges fail to meet by ¼ inch. Fold the first fold to ¼ inch shy of the narrower layer. Baste ¼ inch from the second fold.

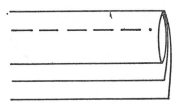

Wadding strip

With a single strand of basting thread, backstitch the strip of wadding to the sleeve side of the armhole seam allowance above the front and back notches, matching the basting in the strip to the earlier backstitches around the armhole. (Identify the front and back notches by the outer cloth seam allowances: one above the notches, where you pressed the seam open; two below.)

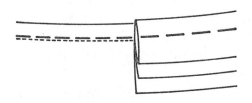

Armhole with wadding strip

From the lining scraps, cut four pieces in the general shape of the illustration, about 5 inches wide and 3¼ inches high at the center, for PERSPIRATION SHIELDS.

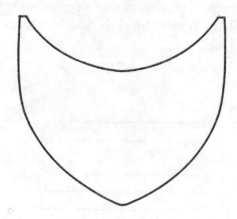

Perspiration shield

Stitch each two pieces together around the two sides. Turn the shields right side out and press. Match the upper (concave) edge of each shield to the coat side of the armhole at the underarm and baste.

Turn under ½ inch around the armhole edge of the sleeve lining and baste. Match the top of the sleeve lining to the coat armhole and baste, just covering the white backstitches. Fell, using two strands of silk thread and tiny ladder stitches.

Lift the perspiration shields about midway of their length and catch their bottom layer to the coat lining.

Fell the lining at the shoulder seams and around any vent. At the neck, at center back, cross stitch about the first 1½ inches of the lining tuck, ending with a small bartack of the same thread. (Illustration on next page).

At the bottom of the coat and sleeves, turn up the lining fold at the basting and fell the bottom layer of the lining, leaving the outer layer free for ease.

Beginning at the bottom of the bridle line and working with the facing side up, work a simple backstitch ¼ inch from the edge of the revers and collar in two strands of silk thread. Take each stitch only about a thread's width behind the previous one and as deep

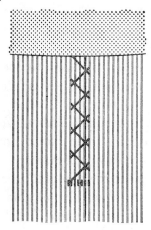

Securing the lining tuck

as possible without going through to the underside. Take care to make the stitches as nearly invisible as possible, pulling each one to the tightness at which it most nearly disappears.

With the coat side up, work the same stitch from the bottom of the bridle line down at least as far as the end of the front facing. If the outer cloth needs the extra flattening, continue around the hemline.

Even though the $1\frac{1}{16}$-inch keyhole cam, which is standard with most buttonhole attachments, is too long for the coat BUTTON-HOLES, you can still use it: Machine work a buttonhole in a scrap and measure it against a coat button. Start the buttonholes in the coat at the cam position that results in the correct length. Once around is sufficient for a foundation and guide for the hand working.

Clean off all the bastings except the one in the lining tuck at center back. Close the pocket openings and the buttonholes with basting in preparation for PRESSING.

A first press is much more complex than subsequent ones, and it is something you should have done rather than attempting it yourself. A person skilled in first presses is found only where coats are made, not at a dry cleaning or alteration shop. Even outlets for made-to-measure clothes are not involved in the first press. If you can find a tailor in your vicinity, go to him. If not, seek a recommendation from a tailor's supply house, and mail your coat out of town if necessary to have the first press done right. After the pressing, take out the last bastings and sew on the BUTTONS.

Given the proper CARE, a well-made coat remains new-looking for years. After each wearing, lightly brush the coat and hang it on a thick, curved hanger—wood or plastic, not wire. Do everything you can to postpone dry cleaning, which is extremely hard on a coat. With good care a coat should not require cleaning any oftener than once a year. Save a few scraps of lining fabric so after a few years you can replace the perspiration shields.

These instructions are equally applicable to OVERCOATS and topcoats. The techniques are the same. But the materials are heavier and the buttons larger, so be sure to specify when you order trimmings.

For a first coat, I have recommended an all-wool cloth in at least a medium weight. MAN-MADE fibers and blends, and very LIGHTWEIGHT outer cloths require pattern changes to regulate fullness. Fold out fullness in the sleeve cap until the seam above the front and back notches is no more than an inch longer than the coat armhole to which it will be matched. Reduce the shoulder width of the back to ¼ inch more than the front. And, in putting together the coat pieces, make the seams about $\frac{1}{16}$ inch deeper than in heavier cloth.

In LEATHER the fullness must be reduced still further. The absolute maximum for sleeve cap fullness is ¾ inch. Alterations in leather are impossible because perforations are permanent, so the pattern must first be verified in cloth. Pinning and basting are out, because of the perforations, but masking tape is a workable substitute. The construction has to be flat; there is no shaping of the coat foundation.

Machine stitching in leather requires a special "leather needle" (sometimes called "narrow-wedge"), which cuts a hole instead of tearing it, as ordinary and ballpoint needles do. The needle should be the smallest that will accommodate the thread, which can be either silk (in the thinner leather) or cotton/polyester. The pressure on the machine presser bar should be reduced to take the extra thickness of leather. The machine stitch is longer than in cloth, 7 to 10 stitches per inch. Seams are finger-pressed open, and the seam allowance is glued down at each side of the seam with rubber cement (which is flexible) for flatness. Hems are glued without sewing.

The limiting factor with leather may well be the cost of cleaning. Many dry cleaners will not accept garments containing leather, and many that do shouldn't. Before you sew very much leather, you may want to locate an establishment that cleans leather competently and at a reasonable price.

CHAPTER 10

Shirts and More

Especially after a coat, it is encouraging to make something that can be cut out and finished the same day. Shirts qualify. In fact, second and subsequent shirts require only about two to four hours.

A key to speed in sewing is the ORDER OF CONSTRUCTION. The instruction sheets that come with patterns must be in a logical order for the sake of understanding. How would you like to make a shirt for the first time by instructions that jump around like this:

> Join the two halves of the collar with the underlining. Stitch the first seam of each sleeve placket. Fold the pockets at the top, right sides together, and stitch the sides. Join cuffs to their facings and underlinings. Stitch the yoke and its facing to the back.

And yet that is exactly the way an expert proceeds, with the sequence depending on whatever happens to be on top of the stack of cut-out pieces.

It is impressive to watch a tailor sit down to the pieces for an entire suit (count them sometime) and stitch his way through without hesitation. Such a feat requires either a lot of practice or a phenomenal memory. But shirt making has so few steps that one or two repetitions commit them to memory.

The most efficient order then is a random one: Stitch everything to the point of pressing; take it all to the pressing board, and press your way through. With a shirt, three or four trips suffice.

Of course there are other ways of making the job faster. High on the list is planning ahead to avoid unnecessary trimming. Time spent in MODIFYING THE PATTERN is time saved on every shirt you make.

Shirt making has been gradually simplified over the years. At one time, flat-felled seams were standard; now they are a sometime thing. A few years ago, french seams appeared briefly in dress shirts, but now simple overcasting predominates.

If you intend to finish the armhole and side seams (including the sleeves) by OVERCASTING, trim the pattern to ¼-inch seam allowance there, first transferring the armhole notches (on front and sleeve) to the seam line so they won't be lost.

Preserve the neckline notches the same way, and reduce the neck seam allowance (on the front, the collar, and both sides of the collar stand) to ¼ inch for ease of construction. Cut the shirt front 1⅞ inches outside center front, and write on the pattern, "Left side only, cut away 1⅛ inches." Cut the left front band (one only) 2½ inches wide. Note that center front is midway of the band (for matching cloth designs), and write on the band pattern, "Cut interfacing 1½ inches."

If you want speed at a sacrifice of some quality, you can reduce to ¼ inch the seam allowance at the yoke bottom and upper back, the shoulders, and the three outer edges of the collar and cuffs. On those seams, however, it is better to retain the ⅝-inch seam allowance and, after stitching, trim to graded widths for extra flatness.

It would be nice if the pattern companies would get the knack of providing NOTCHES where they are helpful and omitting them where they are not. On a shirt pattern, the only notches of value are those at the *armhole* and *neckline*. (And neckline notches would be better matched to the shoulder seams.) In addition, notches should be cut at *center back* (collar, collar stand, yoke, and top of back), *center front* (neckline and hem), the armhole end of the *shoulder* line (yoke and sleeve), the sides of *pockets* at the fold line, and at the limits of any *pleats* or *gathers*. The bottom of the sleeve normally needs no notches, but the placket should be identified by being partially cut.

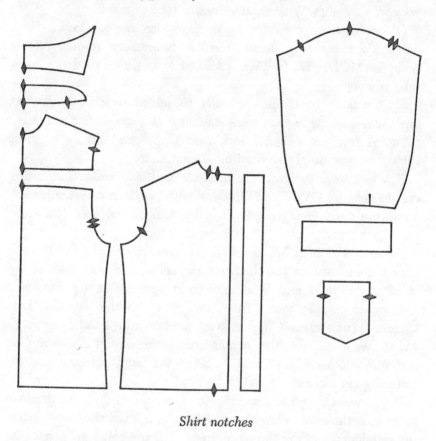

Shirt notches

Pocket placement can be indicated by pins on the shirt front, and no further MARKING of the cloth pieces is called for.

After you have made a few shirts—enough to be sure of the fitting refinements—a more-or-less PERMANENT PATTERN of muslin or *heavy* nonwoven interfacing is a big time saver. Either material can be marked on, and both cling to the cloth without pins or weights. Write on the pattern the amounts of your seam allowances and the required yardage in each of the most common cloth widths. For storage, roll the pieces together instead of subjecting them to repeated folding and unfolding. That way too they are ready for cutting out without pressing.

At the armholes a plain ¼-inch seam with the edges overcast

together is nearly always satisfactory, though in harsher fabrics it is best covered with rayon bias seam binding. At the side seams, in lightweight fabrics FRENCH SEAMS may be preferable to over-casting. For a french seam, cut out at ⅜ inch. Stitch at ⅛ inch, *right sides out*. Press the seam open, turn right sides together, and stitch at ¼ inch.

French seam

For a FLAT-FELLED SEAM cut out at ⅛ inch on the back side and ½ inch on the front. Stitch right sides out and back side up, having the back ⅜ inch away from the front.

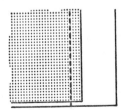

Press both seam allowances toward the back. Tuck under the edge of the front, and stitch.

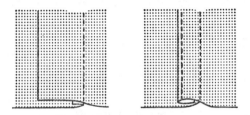

Flat-felled seam

At the armhole it makes little difference whether you fell toward the sleeve or away from it, though I favor working toward it because the shirt-side seam allowance is less full and therefore easier to fell. To flat fell toward the sleeve, cut out the sleeve cap at ⅛ inch and the shirt armhole at ½ inch.

There are so many PLAID shirts that I probably would be negligent if I ignored them. Matching plaids is a 1-2-3 proposition, with the placement of each piece depending on a previous one. The front is 1, the back 2, etc. Usually the effect is more pleasing if center front and center back are located midway between prominent stripes, while the sleeve is usually centered on a stripe. Because of its prominence, the front sleeve notch is a matching point, and it works well on a stripe since that provides a definite pattern to match to. The back merges with the front at the side seam. The yoke is matched to the sleeve at the shoulder, and the collar and collar stand to the yoke, with the collar aligned horizontally for its best appearance at the front.

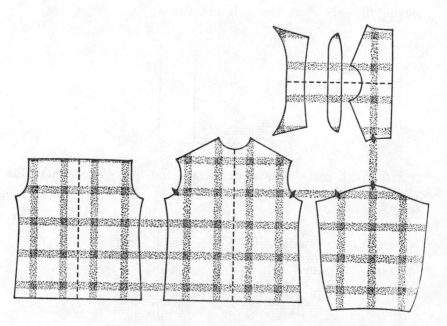

Matching plaid

When a cloth design has a right and a left, the design should move across the shirt front without interruption. Decide how you want the pattern to be centered, and cut one half of the front. Lay that half over an identical spot on the cloth, and note (with pins) the locations of the center front notches. Turn the first-cut half over, and cut the second with the center front notches at the same spots.

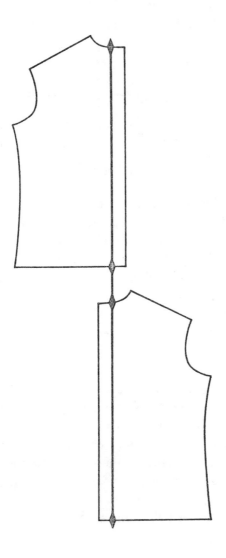

When it comes to joining two cloth pieces of matched cloth design TOP BASTING is the answer. The "top" refers to the fact that you baste with the right side up so you can see what you are doing. Turn under the seam allowance of one side and place it over the other side, design matched. Bring the needle straight up through all three layers at the edge of the fold. For each stitch, introduce the needle into the single layer of cloth opposite where the thread emerges (as in a ladder stitch), run forward underneath, and come *straight* up through three thicknesses at the edge of the fold.

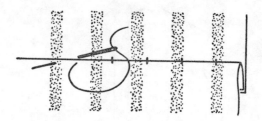

Top basting

Take the stitches as long as the needle easily permits. For stitching, open out the folded side so the two are right sides together (normal stitching position), and follow the basting. Keep top basting in mind too for setting in curved yokes (western style) when outside stitching is undesirable.

In judging the appearance of a garment, the emphasis should be on the outside—on what is seen when the garment is being worn. Attention to inside finishing should never be at the expense of this first consideration. An example of misguided workmanship is the unnecessary binding of seams, which adds ridges to show through to the outside. Another is lining to hide seam allowances that would never be seen, when underlining results in a smoother outside look. The manufacturers of expensive ready-made clothing often cater to ignorance of these facts. Never lose sight of the first criterion of good tailoring: inconspicuous seams, flat and without ridges.

With that preamble let's turn to INTERFACING—where, with what, and how.

The areas of a shirt that should be interfaced are the collar, collar stand, cuffs, and left center front.

Interfacing should strengthen without imposing an unclothlike character. Rigidity is undesirable. On this basis, the preference lies with a woven material, cut in the same direction as the area it reinforces. For a shirt it is seldom necessary to buy fabric that is labeled "interfacing," which is often higher priced due to its brand name. All that is necessary is that the fiber content be compatible with the outer cloth for cleaning and that the interfacing be lighter in weight than the outer cloth. The scraps from one shirt may well interface another.

In all but the heavier shirts, the thickness of a layer of interfacing is little enough to allow its being incorporated into the seam. The method is simple underlining—of the outer half to locate the seam allowances behind the interfacing for a smoother outside look.

For the collar, collar stand, and cuffs, cut the interfacing to the same size and shape as the outer cloth. With the collar stand, simply lay the interfacing against the inside of what will be the outer half, and set them aside to be treated as one piece of cloth when the time comes. Lay out the pieces of the COLLAR and CUFFS, right sides together and outer half on top. Lay the interfacing over them. At the corners, cut away the interfacing to remove unneces-

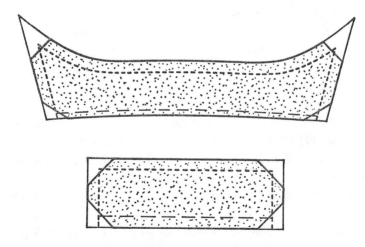

Underlining collar and cuffs

sary bulk. Stitch the three layers together, having the interfacing uppermost for visibility.

Once the interfacing has been included in a seam, don't kid yourself that trimming it close will do anything to minimize its thickness. On the contrary, reflect that its seam allowance is the outermost one, as well as the thinnest. Seam allowances should be graded with the widest toward the outside, so each one covers the edge of the narrower one beneath it.

Turn the stitched pieces (collar and cuffs) over, and trim first the seam allowance of the facing-side outer cloth, as narrow as is practical. Trim next that of the topside outer cloth, a little wider. And last trim the interfacing wider still.

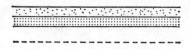

Beveling the seam allowances

A very bad practice that is widely advocated is the "notching" of seam allowances on a curve, as in a rounded cuff. V-shaped sections are cut out of the seam allowance at intervals. To be effective such cuts would have to be deep enough to weaken the seam. But the worst result is that, unless the cut sides meet perfectly after turning, the seam allowance is left with both gaps and laps. At a gap the thickness is three layers, while at a lap it is nine —too much variation for anything but a lumpy seam.

The narrowest seam allowance requires no clipping at curves, and the medium width little if any. The widest should be clipped (not notched) at intervals but not at the same spots as the medium one. The seam thickness then varies only one layer.

For heavier shirts (wool, corduroy, etc.) it is nice to have on hand some of the lightest weight hymo from a tailor's supply. In the interest of flat seams, it is obviously best that a material as thick as hymo be kept out of a seam. So cut out heavier interfacings to finished size (no seam allowance) so they will reach *to* the seam but not *into* it. In the case of hymo interfacings for a shirt (but not a coat), observe a crosswise grainline in cutting out, due to the greater stability of hymo in that direction.

Whenever you cut interfacings to finished size, tailor baste each to the inside of the topside half of outer cloth, and join the two pieces of outer cloth by stitching just outside the interfacing. Leave in the basting until after the topstitching, which will effectively anchor the interfacing.

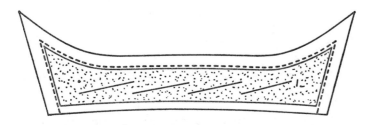

When topstitching is to be omitted, there are two good ways to secure heavier interfacing. One is by the custom touch of the same hand-finishing stitch used around the edge of a coat. And the other, for velvet-like cloths on which any outside sewing would be offensive, is to extend the outline of the interfacing with strips of rayon hem tape (woven edge, not bias). Lap the interfacing onto strips of the hem tape and stitch.

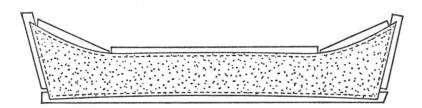

Place the smooth (untaped) side against the inside of the topside outer cloth. Join the two pieces of outer cloth by stitching just outside the interfacing in the tape.

Press open the seams around the collar and cuffs and turn them right side out. If the collar has very sharp points, you can pull them out with the help of a knotted strand of button-and-carpet thread. With the collar still right sides together as stitched, slip the threaded needle inside and take a stitch out at the point. Take one stitch back to the inside over the seam allowance and pull the thread. The knot is then on the outside for easy removal.

Topstitch the collar. Place the two pieces of the COLLAR STAND right sides together with the collar between, and join them in a ¼-inch seam, starting and stopping ¼ inch from the unstitched side.

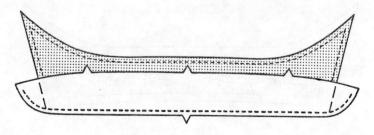

Joining collar to collar stand

In uncooperative cloth this last seam can be accomplished in two steps: First join the collar to either piece of the collar stand. Then add the other piece and stitch again, following the first seam.

Trim the facing-side seam allowance slightly, press open the seam, and turn the collar stand right side out.

In remembering how to finish CENTER FRONT, the figure to keep in mind is the 1½-inch band width. The buttonholes are in the middle of the band: It follows that the finished edge of the front is ¾ inch outside center front.

On the *right* shirt front, turn back the edge at ¾ inch outside center front. Fold under ¼ inch of the turnback, and stitch. Note

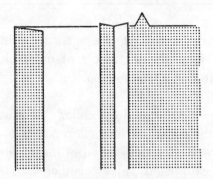

Attaching left center front band

that the result is three layers of cloth at center front, where the buttons will be sewn.

Join the right side of the band to the wrong side of the *left* shirt front in a ¼-inch seam. Press open the seam, and press a ½-inch fold in the outer edge of the band.

Place the band interfacing against the inside of the band under the seam allowances. Turn the band to the outside of the shirt, and topstitch ¼ inch from each side.

Make and attach the POCKETS early in the construction. Don't forget to reinforce each end of the openings with a patch of linen tape on the underside of the shirt front. If the pockets are curved, first stitch around the corners at the seam line (in the single thickness) to make it easier to turn under the seam allowance in a smooth curve.

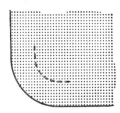

Place the YOKE and its facing right sides together. Sandwich the back between them with its right side toward the yoke, and stitch the joining seam. Press the yoke and the facing up. Topstitch or not.

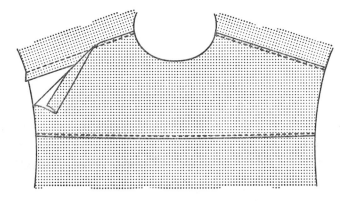

Join the right side of the yoke facing to the wrong side of each shirt front at the shoulder. Press both seam allowances toward the yoke. On the yoke, turn under the shoulder seam allowance and topstitch over the first shoulder seam.

To discourage stretching of the neck the COLLAR/COLLAR STAND should be attached as soon as possible after completion of the shoulder seams and center front. Along the unstitched side of the *facing* half of the collar stand, turn under ¼ inch and press or baste to hold the crease. Join the *outer* half of the collar stand to the shirt neck, right sides together, in a ¼-inch seam. Press the seam allowance up. Baste the turned-under edge of the collar stand facing over the seam. From the outside, stitch all around the collar stand about ⅟₁₆ inch from the edge.

A traditional SLEEVE PLACKET is a professional touch that requires very little effort. For the underlap (back) side, cut a plain rectangle 6 inches long and 1½ inches wide. For the overlap, cut a piece 7 by 2½ inches. At one side of the top, cut away a square inch. Trim the projection to a point.

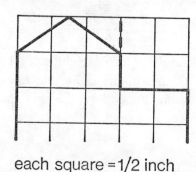

each square = 1/2 inch

Sleeve placket overlap

With everything right side down, join the facings to the sleeve in a ¼-inch seam at each side of the placket cut, stopping ½ inch before the top. Turn up ¼ inch at the opposite side of each facing and at the point of the overlap, and press. (First illustration page 185.)

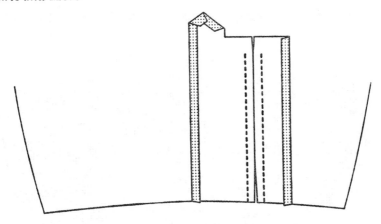

Attaching the sleeve placket facings

Press each facing over its seam allowance. In the sleeve extend the placket cut to ½ inch below the ends of the seams, and from that point cut diagonally up to the last stitch in each seam.

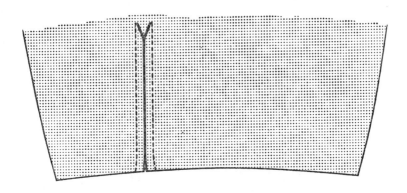

Cutting the sleeve placket

Turn up (to the topside) the little triangle of cloth thus formed. Bring the facings through to the outside, and stitch the folded edge of each (beginning with the underlap) so it just covers the first seam.

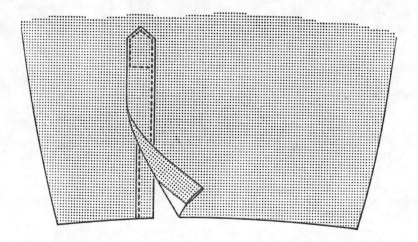

Whenever you have a cloth design to which you want to match the sleeve placket, cut the point of the overlap facing on a line ¼ inch to the back side of the placket cut.

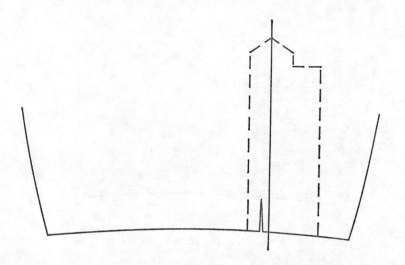

In SLEEVE insertion an outside curve (the sleeve cap) is matched to an inside one (the armhole). The wider the seam allowance, the greater the difference in length of the two cut edges that are to be matched. Reducing the seam allowance to ¼ inch minimizes the problem by making the two lengths nearly equal.

Match each sleeve to its armhole at the beginning of the seam only, and start stitching.

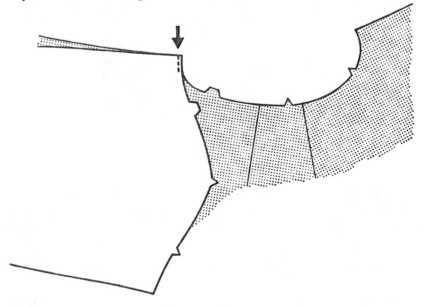

Setting in the sleeve

Place the sleeve cap around the armhole as you stitch, verifying the match at each of the check points (front and back notches, shoulder, and end of seam). Trim away the notches and finish the seam by overcasting or whatever method you have chosen.

Stitch each SIDE SEAM and close the sleeve in one continuous seam.

Join the outer half of each CUFF (with underlining) to the sleeve, right sides together and centers matched. If this is the first time you have made up the pattern, try on the shirt and check sleeve length before you trim the seam allowance. You can still lengthen the sleeve as much as ¾ inch (⅜ from sleeve and ⅜ from cuff).

On the facing half of the cuff turn under the seam allowance and pin or baste it in line with the seam. From the outside, stitch about ¹⁄₁₆ inch on the cuff side of the seam, including the facing underneath. Topstitch the ends and bottom of the cuff ¼ inch from the edge.

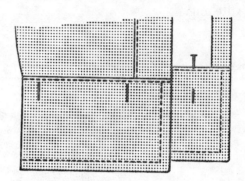

Or, if you are avoiding topstitching, turn under a little less than the full seam allowance on the cuff facing and pin or baste it to cover the seam by about ⅟₁₆ inch. From the outside, stitch within the seam, including the facing underneath.

Finish the BOTTOM of the shirt with a narrow machine-stitched hem.

Machine work BUTTONHOLES in the center of the left front band, on the overlap side of the cuffs, and one horizontally in the collar stand on the left.

Shirt BUTTONS can be sewn on quickly with a zigzag machine. And they are as secure as hand-sewn ones provided the threads are pulled to the underside and tied. Stitch over a pin so the buttons will stand away from the shirt, and leave the pin in place until after the threads have been tied.

The styling of men's shirts has gone wild. A traditional pattern invites countless VARIATIONS.

The simplest involve no more than drawing a line across a pattern piece to add a seam. That piece is cut out as two with a seam allowance on each. An example is the addition of a FRONT YOKE, which may be cut from a contrasting cloth such as suede or scraps from the pants with which the shirt is to be worn.

If the front yoke seam is placed just above the pocket line, a pocket flap can be enclosed in the seam.

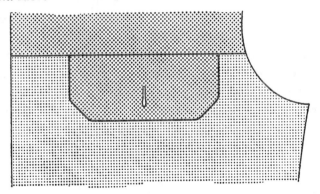

Front yoke enclosing pocket flap

In heavier cloth the facing side of the pocket flap should be cut from a thinner lining fabric, as should the facing half of the yoke and the collar stand, if any.

In another variation the back yoke is eliminated and the front and back joined at the NATURAL SHOULDER line. Draw in the shoulder line on the yoke pattern, and match the yoke pattern to the front and back at the seam lines. Cut both front and back all

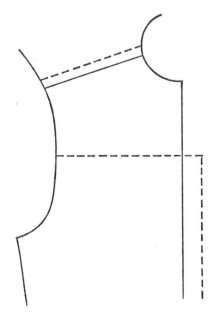

Deleting the yoke

the way to the shoulder, adding a seam allowance to each and dropping any fullness in the back at center back.

For SLIPOVER styles the shirt front is cut on a center front fold. One possibility then is to omit the collar and trim the neckline in whatever shape appeals to you: an oval, a V, a square. Front and back neckline facings are cut from the same or contrasting cloth. The facings are joined at the shoulders and attached to either the underside or the outside of the shirt neck.

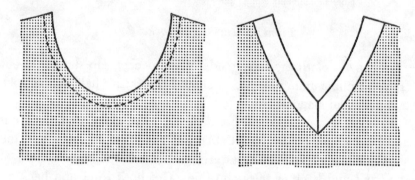

Necklines for collarless slipover shirts

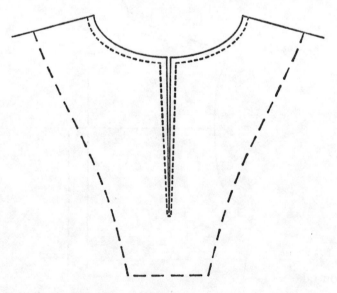

Neckline facing with placket

An alternative is to retain the original neckline, either with or without a collar, and add a partial opening at center front. The opening can be finished with a facing which allows the shirt to be worn open at the neck. (See bottom of page 190.)

In this style you can avoid decreasing the neck size by cutting out the shirt front on a fold a seam's width outside center front. The end of the placket should be reinforced with a few narrow zigzag stitches or hand overcasting before the seam is pressed open and turned right side out. Fasteners can be a zipper, eyelets and laces, or cloth loops and buttons.

A collar can be attached directly to the shirt neckline without a separate collar stand. The collar neckline follows the collar stand pattern, with the end seams back ¾ inch from the seam lines on the collar stand pattern.

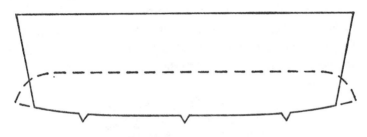

Collar without collar stand

Another way to finish a neckline opening is like a traditional sleeve placket. Turn the shirt front upside down, start the cut at center front, and face the sides of the opening with an underlap and an overlap cut from your sleeve placket pattern in whatever length you need. Face the neckline edges with a narrow bias strip.

PATTERN JUGGLING is a good way to get the design you want. Sleeves and collars can be interchanged between patterns provided the patterns are the same size and the same general type: shirts designed to be worn next to the body, unlined shirts/jackets meant to be worn over shirts, or heavier jackets and coats that are lined.

If you take a sleeve or collar from a pattern, of course you must also adopt the armhole or neckline for which it was drafted. Align the two patterns by matching center fronts (or backs) and the shoulder lines.

In looking to ready-mades for INSPIRATION, don't ignore the cheaper, mass-produced clothes, which are often (over) loaded with style gimmicks. Their details, translated tastefully in good materials, can result in outstanding one-of-a-kind garments.

The great variety of FABRICS used in men's clothes today call for a large repertoire of handling skills.

The heavily NAPPED fabrics (velvet, corduroy) require a steam iron and a needleboard. Makeshifts, such as using a piece of the same fabric as a press cloth, leave velvet-like garments with an unfinished look. The pile on the seam allowances must be smashed, and the only way to do that without damaging the outside surface is to press against a needleboard.

Seams should be as few as possible, and topstitching is better omitted. In the firmer fabrics the outer edge of collars and cuffs can be cut on a fold. Sleeve plackets can be made with a patch-type facing stitched to the right side of the garment, which is then cut and the facing turned to the underside.

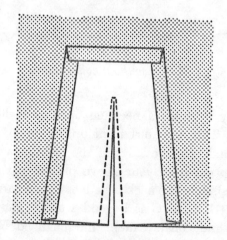

Patch-type facing for sleeve placket

The firmer velveteens and corduroys are not hard to handle. But velours are prone to stretch, especially in crosswise or bias seams. Loosen the pressure on the machine presser bar and *push* the cloth through the machine. If you are still unable to control the stretching, you can resort to the old trick of stitching through tissue paper: Lay a strip of paper over where the seam is to go, and stitch. Afterward tear away the paper.

The adjustment of pressure on the presser bar is not a delicate one. Firm, medium, or loose is exact enough. You can gauge the setting by noting the force with which the presser foot snaps down when you lower it (protect the feed mechanism by having cloth under the presser foot before you test). This adjustment is a big factor in stitching control.

In KNITS it is only the single knits that require special handling. The finer ones pucker, the heavier ones stretch, and the medium weights are unpredictable. Both extremes call for a lighter pressure on the machine presser bar—the heavier ones to make room for the extra thickness and the delicate ones to prevent marring by the feed mechanism.

The thread to choose for knits is cotton/polyester, and for the extreme lightweights there is a lingerie-weight thread. Put in a new machine needle. A fine ballpoint is best, but the "new" is even more important than the type because the least bit of roughness snags a knit. (A ballpoint needle is just a smoothly dull one. An ordinary, sharp needle pierces the strands of knits, causing them to break and run; while a ballpoint is more likely to go safely between strands.)

Some of the newer sewing machines are capable of seaming knits in one stitching that includes overcasting of the ⅛-inch seam. The technique works well on the stabler doubleknits. But on the less cooperative single knits, stitching so close to the edge is exacting. And so narrow a seam allowance does not permit stretching the cloth while stitching, to prevent puckering.

The way to take the strain out of sewing on single knits is to stitch the seams in two stages. Cut out at ⅝ inch if there is any possibility of puckering. The slick jerseys and tricots (which are the most likely to pucker) are easier to cut on a rough cloth surface. Stitch with a narrow zigzag—narrow enough that it almost passes for a straight stitch and wide enough to result in a seam with as much "give" as the cloth. The stitch should be short, about 15 per inch.

Trim to ⅛ inch. Leave the stitch length and the machine tension the same, but switch to a wide zigzag and overcast the seam. As you know, the tension is normally decreased for a wide zigzag. Leaving the tension higher than normal causes the seam allowance to be snugged in neatly. Complete each seam before you go to the next.

Linting is a problem in sewing knits, especially those of man-made fibers because of static electricity. Brush out around the bobbin frequently. If the fabric lints so badly that thread breaking becomes an annoyance, try increasing the upper tension slightly.

When thread breaks, the tendency is to think the tension is too high, but often the opposite is the case. Especially in older machines, where the thread grooves have become worn, it is important that the bobbin thread be caught up smartly by the upper thread. If the tension is loose, the thread is allowed to develop slack as the stitch is formed—which leads to snagging.

In spite of their idiosyncrasies, knits are a joy to sew. Their stretchiness makes fitting less critical. Patterns designed for knits have fewer seams and fewer openings. There is no interfacing. The tiny, neat seams make possible dozens of shortcuts in construction. For example, a cuff can be a single rectangle, folded at the bottom and the double edge sewn to the flat sleeve. The seam that closes the sleeve extends to the bottom of the cuff.

Collars too can be cut in one and the double edge sewn to the *underside* of the neckline. The seam, on the outside, is hidden by the collar.

A pattern that has been drafted for woven cloth or doubleknits

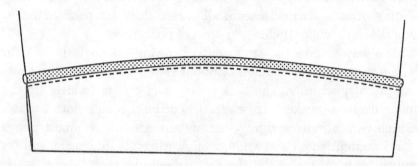

Piped sleeve bottom

is too loose made up in a single knit. But in SLEEPWEAR that is what you want. An ordinary shirt pattern can be the basis for knit sleepwear.

If you want the sleeves to be loose at the bottom, reshape them to take a plain hem or perhaps a facing to the outside with piping.

PIPING is a popular sleepwear trim that can be easily made up. Rough-cut a bias strip of the trimming fabric, enclose in it a pre-shrunk string or washable yarn, and stitch fairly close to the string using a zipper presser foot.

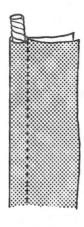

Piping

Trim the double edge to the width of your seam allowance. Match the raw edges of piping and facing right sides together, and stitch closer to the string than before.

Sew the right side of the facing to the underside of the sleeve. Turn the facing to the outside, covering the seam allowances, and sew the piped edge to the sleeve, stitching either near or within the piping seam.

To enclose piping in a seam, for example around a collar, join it first to either half. Then add in the other half and stitch again, following the first stitches.

SWEATER KNITS require a slightly different technique. Cut out at ¼ inch outside the seam lines. Have the pressure on the presser bar very loose, and push the cloth through the machine.

An almost-straight stitch does not have enough "give" for a sweater knit: Use a medium-width zigzag for the first stitching. Trim to even the edges, and overcast with a wide zigzag. Steam press each seam immediately to shrink out the stretch.

Ribbing does not need to be measured. Rough-cut a folded strip and steam press the crease. For a test, trim the double edge at a width of about ½ inch more than you would for the garment. Apply the strip to a scrap of the knit, stretching the ribbing firmly over the scrap as you stitch. When you have learned how hard to pull for the results you want, cut away the seam and retrieve the test strip for use. Ribbing varies extremely in its ability to stretch and recover. The force with which it is stretched during application is therefore a much more reliable guide than a tape measure.

Ribbing works well also in combination with woven cloth. And it makes construction so easy that the temptation is to overuse it. In a sleeveless top with ribbed neck, armholes, and bottom, the order of construction is:

> Stitch one shoulder seam.
> Apply ribbing to the neckline.
> Stitch the other shoulder seam.
> Apply ribbing to both armholes.
> Close one side seam.
> Add ribbing to the bottom.
> Close the other side seam.

And the top is finished.

To apply ribbing to a pointed neckline, begin precisely at center front leaving a little extra length of ribbing. Tack the stitches and proceed around the neck, stopping a few inches before you get back to center front. Anchor the first end of the ribbing to the other side of the neckline, and trim. Complete the neckline stitching. Add the second end of ribbing to the other side of the neck as you did the first.

The new availability of materials and patterns puts just about everything a man wears within the compass of home sewing. A recent addition is the one-piece JUMP SUIT or coveralls. Fitting a jump suit is a good example of working out pattern changes.

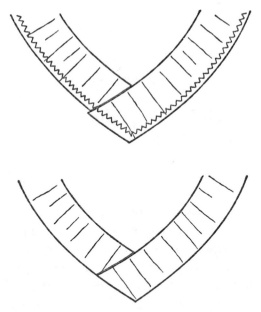

A pointed neckline with ribbing, underside (above) and outside

The first time you make up the pattern, lengthen or shorten it an exact amount based on your observation of ready-mades. But cut out with a waistline seam, adding a wide seam allowance (say an inch). Make the top, make the bottom, and machine baste (just a long stitch with loosened tension) the two together at the waist with the seam to the *outside*. Try on the suit and verify the body length before permanently stitching the waist. Cover the seam with a lengthwise band stitched to the outside—most jump suits are designed with waistbands anyway. The next time you make a one-piece suit, you will know how to adjust the pattern so you can cut to size without a waistline seam.

Two-way zippers are not readily available. For a jump suit buy two ordinary zippers, one the correct length and the other the shortest (cheapest) length available. (The best weight is a so-called light jacket zipper.) Remove the slide from the short zipper, and add it to the bottom of the long one to make a zipper that opens from both ends.

CHAPTER 11

Going On from Here

The biggest surprise men's tailoring had for me was its nature. I had envisioned it as a strange system into which one had to be initiated by a magical process. Instead it turned out to be no mystery at all, but a simple collection of efficient steps that go together to make sewing the happy experience it should be. Mastering these steps, and applying the same businesslike approach to organizing tools and projects, frees precious time.

The TIME you have to devote to sewing is of three kinds. There are the extended, uninterrupted periods, which are the only ones that most people utilize. There are the scattered bits of time in the five- to ten-minute range that are the extra resource of very productive people. And there are the overlapping occasions, when the portable details of sewing can be combined with other activities.

The only part of sewing that requires the first kind of time is the planning and cutting out. If that time is limited, it should not be squandered on other operations. Whenever you cut out, make a day of it. Cut as many things as you have cloth and ideas for, and assemble all the components. Cut the interfacings, find the appropriate thread, and invent the decorative touches. Write yourself a note about any plans that are not obvious, and stack everything together beside the sewing machine.

A scrapbook of small-project ideas will serve on cutting-out days as a prompter for the imaginative use of scraps. Once the pieces are cut out the project is well on its way, ready for completion on a day when you have more time.

The bits and pieces of time are for machine work, and they should not be wasted on what can be done away from the machine and the iron. At any time, you should have enough cut out to be able to stitch for a quarter of an hour without getting up. And with hesitation banished, that is a lot of stitching. The incoming stack becomes two outgoing ones: one for pressing and one for hand work. When the incoming stack disappears, it is replenished by a visit to the iron.

Overlapping occasions are an opportunity to combine sewing with other forms of needlework for really great and personal creations that money can't buy. Knitting, crochet, needlepoint, embroidery, appliqué, macramé—all are priceless complements for sewing. And they don't consume time of the first order.

What a deplorable waste it is to think you must finish what you have started before taking on something new! It is only by being prepared with projects in every stage of development that you can make the most of all three kinds of sewing time.

The CONVENIENCE of a sewing center depends mostly on accessibility of the machine. You can largely offset the handicap of isolation of the pressing site, and it makes no difference at all where you cut out. But you must be able to get to the machine quickly if you are to take advantage of those stray five and ten minutes. The ideal location for the sewing machine is the most lived-in spot in the house, even at the cost of separation from the other sewing stations.

A sewing machine requires so little to be ready to go: a good light, a chair of its own, a wastebasket. Provide a dust cover for the machine head so the cabinet can remain open. Restrict clutter to absolute essentials: scissors, ripper, thimble, pins. Anchor the pin box to save time and temper. Hand needles should be within reach in a fixed pin cushion. Basting thread too should be secured, with the end free for easy grabbing.

Orderliness can be the very thing that stands in the way of efficiency. Because cutting out, stitching, pressing, and hand work take place at some distance from each other, tools too must be scattered for convenience. If you cut out at a dining table, find a drawer nearby for shears, pins, chalk, and tape measure. Each "station" should be equipped so no time is lost in running back and forth.

At the machine, tool storage needs division. There are strictly machine accessories and those that are useful in hand work as well. The double-duty tools call for portable housing: a removable drawer, a removable partitioned tray within a drawer. Duplication of tools may be an economy. The machine essentials should have their counterparts in the double-duty group so the originals never leave the machine.

If drawer space at the machine is scarce, a wall shelf mounted at sitting height may solve the problem. An open arrangement can be an asset if it is designed with the aim of providing inspiration. Beware of bulletin boards. Unless they are constantly renewed, bulletin boards become nagging reminders of what has been left undone. A thing of beauty at the stitching center is a more effective invitation—an art object, a plant, an inspired arrangement of sewing tools.

An expense that contributes to storage convenience pays for itself many times over in time saved. Ideal containers are prudent purchases. The qualities to look for in storage are protection, accessibility, and easy identification. As an example of ideal containers, clear plastic bobbin boxes are hard to improve on—one for each kind of thread regularly used.

Supplies can be stored away from the machine if necessary. But try to get them out of closets, out of bags, and into drawers. Sort and classify. Devote a drawer to patterns, another to interfacings and linings, another to zippers and trims. If supplies are misplaced, money as well as time is wasted on unnecessary purchases.

Scraps deserve prime storage space. Don't allow them to be crowded out by full lengths of cloth that are waiting in line to be introduced into the system. If given shallow, orderly storage, scraps are a ready source of gifts and distinctive trims. And they are pure bonus. Turning scraps to account brings the special satisfaction of making ingenuity and energy take the place of money.

Another resource that it pays to organize is information. A REFERENCE center is a treasure house of the most vital ingredient in sewing success. Sewing is not an art; it is a craft—a many faceted craft that is a medium for the art of design. As a craft, sewing can be learned. Information is the magic that transforms a novice into an expert. Books and catalogues are the life force of sewing. Sometimes they teach; sometimes they inspire. Either way they make a necessary contribution.

The first item in the sewing reference center should be the manual for your sewing machine. If the original has been mislaid, write the manufacturer for another. Any public library can supply the address.

Magazines are a major feature of a home library. But to be of value, articles must be extracted and filed for instant access. When you are looking for information, a stack of old magazines is about as helpful as a haystack when you need a needle.

A reference file is a constantly growing part of everyday life. You don't set aside time and make a file. Files are made in the odd moments when you leaf through a magazine while waiting for a pot to boil. Go through a magazine once only—from beginning to end. When you are interrupted, mark the page you have reached so you won't waste time backtracking. Remove articles of interest and put them beside your favorite reading spot, or in your pocket(book) to fill the time you spend waiting somewhere. As you read, underline the essential points so they will stand out without a second complete reading.

Articles of permanent value should be labeled with the name and date of the magazine. Write on them too the general subject under which they will be filed: alterations, knits, leather and fur, pressing, tailoring, wool, etc. It isn't necessary to invent a complete filing system. Just provide a folder for each category of information you have, and the system will materialize.

In spite of all the advertising assurances that it pays to sew, I wonder whether the full importance is appreciated. Sometimes sewing is rated on a par with hobbies whose only end is pleasure or the acquisition of a luxury. And I don't mean to underrate pleasures and luxuries, which make the difference between existing and living. The ability to sew well is a pleasure too. And it makes possible a variety of luxuries. But sewing has a fundamental involvement in the necessities of life: Sewing produces clothing, and it provides an attractive setting for food and shelter.

Anyone who has tried to sew without guidance has found himself mocked by the slogan "sew and save." Sewing in ignorance is better described as "sew and slave."

When the full value of knowledgeable sewing is realized, it is easy to see why the tailors have been such jealous guardians of their special skill.

Index